A
B.R.A.V.E.
YEAR

52 Weeks Being Mindful

by

Gabriel Constans, Ph.D.

A B.R.A.V.E. YEAR
52 Weeks Being Mindful
by
Gabriel Constans, Ph.D.

Second Imprint JC Studio Press 2021

ISBN: 978-1-7398281-2-7
Ebook available.

Jane's
Studio Press

Acknowledgements

I am deeply grateful for all the teachers, students, mentors, and friends, who have influenced, enlightened, challenged, and supported my understanding and practice of mindful meditation. Those that come to mind, and to heart, are Tara Brach, Bob Stahl, Stephen Levine, Bell Hooks, Bruce and Jill Hyman, Rev. Debra Johnson, Alice Walker, Jon Kabat-Zinn, Ajahn Chah, Professor Jane Carr, Jiyu Kennett, Joseph Goldstein, Elaine Cashman, Shunryu Suzuki, Jacques Verduin, Jack Kornfield, and Sylvia Boorstein. Their generosity, understanding, and wisdom, inspire and inform everything I do, say or am. Thank you one and all. I hope this book, and what it has to offer, continues to benefit others with some of the insight and compassion I have received from these kind beings.

Gabriel Constans, Ph.D.

About the Author

When I was sixteen my view of the world, and myself, was transformed with the reading of Be Here Now by Baba Ram Das, and practicing Zen at Mt. Shasta Abby, in Northern California. Over the last 40 years, my journey includes work with mental health and meditation in counseling centers, hospice, bereavement departments, hospitals, businesses, private practice, secondary schools, health and recovery centers, colleges, and post-trauma programs in the U.S. and abroad. For the last ten years, I have been teaching in prisons, jails and detention centers throughout California. There is much that I do not know, and it is in this not knowing that I continue to learn, and offer these teachings on mindful meditation. Please contact me with any questions, concerns, insights, or comments.

Website: www.gogabriel.com
Email: constans@gogabriel.com.

Introduction to a B.R.A.V.E. Year

Before Reacting Access Validate and Explore

There are three reasons these classes in mindfulness use the acronym B.R.A.V.E. First, the acronym is easy to remember, and reminds us to pause, pay attention, acknowledge what is taking place, and look into its ever-changing character. B.R.A.V.E. is a simple mnemonic for mindful meditation. Secondly, it is a brave act to allow oneself to be still, if even for a moment, to look at one's present experience, and not be doing something. Thirdly, it takes courage, bravery, to honestly witness what we discover, inside and out, without turning away or getting caught in the content.

This book has fifty-two sessions, which can be practiced in a series, or individually. Each lesson is a class unto itself. Every unit can also be copied, and provided to students, and/or for use by the teacher, as an outline. If teaching, it has been found best to provide the material to students at the end of class, so they can use it to practice throughout the week, and are not distracted trying to read it during the session. There is no need to "prove" or "believe" that these exercises work. Students, and teachers, are encouraged to use those that resonate, and which they find are making a difference in their daily lives.

Classes can be structured in whatever manner one chooses. For example, one may begin with a description of B.R.A.V.E., or a discussion of what mindful meditation is, then read the short description before each exercise and summarize it in one's own words or understanding. Every exercise, or practice, is described in the second section of this workbook (Exercise Area). The amount of time used for discussion, and the practice of each activity, can vary, depending on how much time is allotted per week. If the weekly session is an hour long, then it is best to spend 5-10 minutes per exercise. If it is a two-hour session then those times can be doubled. If one chooses, you can also make an audio recording (reading) of any of the meditation exercises, step by step, thus making it possible to practice without one's eyes open. If you make a recording, be sure to leave long pauses between each step.

Like the rest of the body, it's good to exercise the mind. Daily exercise, and meditation, has been shown to improve health, by decreasing stress, which allows the body (and mind) to naturally release endorphins, relax and heighten awareness. There is a lot of research on mindfulness and meditation, which have found it to be of great benefit for health and wellbeing. Here are a few significant studies.

Harvard Medical School. 2015. Neuroscientist, Sara Lazar, did brain scans on meditators and found that meditation can literally change the brain, including sensory regions of the brain being enhanced, as well as gray matter in the frontal cortex, which involves memory and decision making, and the amygdala getting smaller, which is the part of the brain associated with anxiety, fear and stress.

A UCLA, 2015 study, discovered that long-term meditators have better preserved brains than non-mediators, as they aged.

Johns Hopkins University, 2014, found 47 well-designed research studies on meditation, that suggest that mindfulness meditation can help reduce pain, depression and anxiety.

Contents

A
B.R.A.V.E.
YEAR

FIFTY-TWO CLASSES

THIS WEEK

Mindful exercises to reduce stress, increase the ability to self-reflect, and learn how to live with internal and external realities. Bringing one's attention, or awareness, to the present moment with intention.

Take a Look Inside
(Exercise Area—There Is—Page 120)

Everything has a stimulus and response. Between stimulus and response there is a space. In that space is our power to choose our response. In our response lie our growth and our freedom.

Vicktor Frankl (psychologist and holocaust survivor).

Try sitting and closing your eyes for a short time. See what happens. Notice anything that comes into awareness, and write it down in your head, as if making a note. "There is… a pain in my butt." "There is… a thought about Mom." "There's… a sound in the other room." "There is… my head nodding off to sleep." Give your inner world some love and attention. There's a lot going on in there.

Any Place. Any Time.
(Exercise Area—Body Check—page 122)

Being mindful isn't something that requires one to sit, cross the legs and close the eyes for long periods of time; though a daily practice of doing such is beneficial. It can be done anywhere, at any time.

After opening the eyes in the morning, take some breaths and check in with yourself before getting up.

While getting dressed, brushing the teeth, or going to the restroom, notice if the mind is already thinking, planning and rehearsing for the day ahead. If so, bring the mind and attention back to the present moment and current activity.

Intend to mindfully listen to, and connect with, those that you live with and encounter throughout the day.

While working, just work. When playing, just play. When learning, just learn. When listening, just listen. Give whatever you are doing your full attention at that moment.

If something needs to be planned or prepared, schedule a time for planning, and during that time make plans and prepare.

THIS WEEK

Mindful exercises to reduce stress, increase the ability to self-reflect, and learn how to live with internal and external realities. Bringing one's attention, or awareness, to the present moment with intention.

Habits and Conditioning
(Exercise Area—What A Thought—page 153)

There are countless habits, and ways of thinking, which tend to dominate our thoughts and actions. With mindfulness, we can begin to identify and observe what some of these habits are. When beginning to meditate, one may not see these habits clearly. As practice continues our conditioning begins to stand out, and is recognized shortly after it arises, before it takes over and we are catapulted into habitual automatic thinking, and reactions.

Habitual Thinking and Self-Talk
(Exercise Area—Points of Contact—page 124)

Common habits of the mind include habitual thinking, and negative self-talk, or interpretations, of thoughts and experiences.

Habitual thinking includes believing the worse possible outcome is always in store. It discounts anything positive and exaggerates the negative. We convince ourselves that we know what other people are thinking or feeling, and why they act the way they do, without any evidence of such. Such thinking also requires us to believe that we are always right, and must defend our actions and opinions. Habitual thinking often involves blaming others, and holding them responsible for a situation, and a personal list of unbreakable rules we impose on self and others.

Negative self-talk is a way of distancing one's self from the reality of an experience, by habitually interpreting and identifying with a thought, or situation, as one's personal responsibility and fault. Examples of negative self-talk include, "I'm worthless." "I'll never get this right." "No one can help me." "Things will never change." "I'm such an idiot." "No one understands me." "I deserve this."

By grounding one's self in the body, and the senses, insight into our minds habits of habitual thinking and negative self-talk is heightened, and we begin to counteract and short-circuit such conditioning, by seeing it clearly, and not getting caught in it. Begin by tuning into the body, and noticing where it is touching, or being touched, by an object, person, or one's self.

THIS WEEK

Mindful exercises to reduce stress, increase the ability to self-reflect, and learn how to live with internal and external realities. Bringing one's attention, or awareness, to the present moment with intention.

Our In-Common Behavior Traits
(Exercise Area—The Reporter—page 126)

What lies behind us and what lies before us are small matters compared to what lies within us.

Ralph Waldo Emerson

To be B.R.A.V.E., is to pay attention moment-to-moment, with nonjudgmental awareness, of whatever is happening in the moment, as it is only in the present moment that we can make changes with the self.

There are three strong behavior traits, which we tend to repeat, believe, think, and act from, without any awareness that we are doing so. Sometimes we shift from one to another, combine several or all three, but tend to function primarily from one trait, as a means of surviving and making sense of our experience and the world. These traits are Villain, Hero, and Victim. They are not good or bad, but the result of habit and conditioning. When we become aware of them, we have more opportunity, choice and freedom.

Villain – Can include thoughts such as:
"I'm tough." "I'm no good." "I'm bad." "Just doing what's been

16

done to me." "I'll get what I want when I want it." "Nobody's going to tell me what to do." "I'll show them!"

Hero – Can include thoughts such as: "I'm here to save you." "I'm in control." "I know what's right and wrong." "I'm the only one." "I want to be admired and looked up to." "I'm strong and powerful." "Look at me."

Victim – Can include thoughts such as: "It's all my fault." "There's nothing I can do." "This always happens to me?" "They made me do it." "It's hopeless." "This is not going to turn out well." "What's the point?" "Why me?"

Which personality traits are most prominent in our lives, and what do we tell ourselves about these traits and thoughts? Be an investigative reporter with the self for a few minutes, and see what you discover.

THIS WEEK

Mindful exercises to reduce stress, increase the ability to self-reflect, and learn how to live with internal and external realities. Bringing one's attention, or awareness, to the present moment with intention.

Remembering to Stop
(Exercise Area—S.T.O.P.—page 127)

There are a number of shortcuts to help us remember to bring awareness to mind. Some of these are acronyms, or abbreviations, like B.R.A.V.E. Once they become familiar, they can be used to pause and see what is going on. S.T.O.P. is one of these tools.

S.T.O.P. stands for Stop – Take a Breath – Observe – Proceed. Whenever we tell ourselves to S.T.O.P. throughout the day, it is a reminder to pause, give attention to the breath, observe what we are experiencing, and then proceed with awareness. There is no limit to the number of times we can use this devise. It can be twice a day, once before each meal, or every hour.

This Is Rare
(Exercise Area— R.A.R.E.—page 129)

Another favorite shortcut that can be practiced is R.A.R.E., which is short for Recognize – Allow – Review – Envision. Whenever we pause, take a breath, and are mindful, we can use the opportunity to clearly decipher what is arising and passing away, without trying to avoid it, push it away, or hold on to it. If we choose, we can also look at what is taking place with a fine toothcomb, and discover cause and effect. Reminding ourselves to recognize what is happening, allowing it to be, and honestly exploring the contents, creates self-acceptance, awareness, and greater choice and understanding. R.A.R.E. provides some distance from the content we are conscious of.

Acronyms Create Space
(Exercise Area— Breath of Life—page 131)

Using these shortcuts, acronyms, and mnemonics, soon become second nature, and provide space to deal with difficult sensations, emotions and thoughts. Observing and allowing what "comes up" does not mean we agree with, or like, everything that arises. By recognizing and "accepting" what is there, we are taking away some of the power such feelings and thoughts may have over our behavior, when we are unaware of them, or trying to avoid them all together.

B.R.A.V.E., S.T.O.P., and R.A.R.E., all begin by bringing awareness to the breath.

THIS WEEK

Mindful exercises to reduce stress, increase the ability to self-reflect, and learn how to live with internal and external realities. Bringing one's attention, or awareness, to the present moment with intention.

Bringing Awareness to Sound
(Exercise Area—Sound Sense—page 133)

Mindfulness helps us see that sensations, emotions and thoughts are transitory. Watch closely, and notice the changing conditions of the senses, including sound. What is discovered is also true about thoughts and emotions. Each moment is different from the last. A sound may increase or decrease in volume, intensity, or duration, several times within a few seconds. It may also seem to stay the same, even though it is never constant, or permanent. Sounds can come from the external or internal environment.

Experiences Are Not Ours to Have and to Hold
(Exercise Area—Breath of Life—page 131)

By tuning into the body, and its senses, we discover that everything comes and goes, and is within a vast continuum. The most direct way to being aware of our emotions and thoughts, and the space within which they come and go, is to bring attention to the breath. The breath brings us to the here and now – the immediate. The air that enters and leaves our bodies is not ours to own or hold. Sensations, emotions and thoughts, are not ours either. We do not own them, and they do not define who we are. When we bring awareness to their existence, we are less likely to believe we can hold them, or own them, any more than we do the air we breathe.

Be Your Own Meteorologist
(Exercise Area—Weather Report—page 145)

There is always enough room in the sky for any type of weather, even hurricanes, typhoons and monsoons. There is enough space for everything to arise and dissipate, to come and go. With mindful meditation, we learn to give attention to our internal weather systems and see that like the earth, our sensations, emotions, and thoughts, also come and go, and exist within a vast space of awareness. Thoughts, emotions, and sensations are not facts, or ultimate truths, but temporary and fluid experiences. Some are stronger than others, but none need define us, or keep us stuck in the mud of inattention and self-identification.

THIS WEEK

Mindful exercises to reduce stress, increase the ability to self-reflect, and learn how to live with internal and external realities. Bringing one's attention, or awareness, to the present moment with intention.

Close the Eyes and See What Happens
(Exercise Area—There Is—page 120)

Don't blink, or you may miss everything. Try keeping your eyes closed for a while and see what happens. What are you aware of? What takes place inside when we pay attention, or bring awareness, to our experience? There is so much going on, that we seldom take the time to notice what it is, let alone identify, or acknowledge, what there is.

Making Sense of What Is Going On
(Exercise Area—S.E.E.I.T.—page 135)

Mindfulness practice can be one of the ways to pause, breathe, stop and look at what is happening. But, what if what we witness, or observe, is overwhelming and/or jumping from one thing to another? What do we do when the sensations, emotions and/or thoughts are arising and passing, seemingly all at once, or in rapid secession?

S.E.E.I.T. can help us label what we experience and encompass most everything, and anything, that may come into our consciousness or awareness. S stands for Senses. E is for Emotion. The second E denotes Emptiness. I is the letter for Intention. And

T is our Thoughts.

Senses include all that can be felt, heard, tasted, smelled, spoken or seen.

Emotions are a spectrum including sadness, joy, grief, pain, laughter, and anger.

Emptiness is when there are no emotions, thoughts, senses or intentions.

Intention arises as desire and/or wishes and motivations.

Thoughts are just that and can be broken down further into P.U.F.F. (P.U.F.F. stands for Past, Unfolding, Fantasy or Future.)

S.E.E.I.T. is a way to remember, a means to slow down, pause and see what is happening in our body moment by moment. It can assist our understanding that what is going on internally and externally is not who we are, but what we are experiencing in the present. It is a step towards not only creating "space" between stimulus and response, but also identifying what happens in that space, and giving us insight and freedom to choose.

THIS WEEK

Mindful exercises to reduce stress, increase the ability to self-reflect, and learn how to live with internal and external realities. Bringing one's attention, or awareness, to the present moment with intention.

Awareness of Habitual Thinking and Actions
(Exercise Area—There Is—page 120)

Reflect on any habitual patterns that may be a result of anxiety or unease. Do you say things you wish you hadn't, or do things without thinking, because you're anxious or fearful? Do you repeat certain actions, or have patterns of behavior, which give temporary relief from worries, a racing mind, or intrusive thoughts, but cause more complications as a result? Most of us do, to varying degrees and depths. Instead of worrying, or buying into our fears and thoughts, be mindful. Awareness of what is taking place, in the moment, can give us freedom from our habitual thinking and behavior.

What Are We Doing and Why
(Exercise Area—Inquiring Mind—page 138)

As we practice, we become more aware of not only the physical sensations within us and other external stimuli, but also our thoughts and emotions. Mindfulness allows us to look inside and see what we are burning and the fuel we are using to burn it. When we react, based on past conditioning, we do not pause, and recognize the space between the stimulus and the response. It is within that space that one can choose to be, or do, something differently. Being mindful helps to see clearly what we are doing and why?

Labeling and Differentiating Our Experience
(Exercise Area—S.E.E.I.T.—page 135)

Mindfulness practice teaches us to pause, breathe, stop and look at what is happening. If what we witness, or observe, is overwhelming and/or jumping from one thing to another, it can be confusing. When sensations, emotions and/or thoughts are arising and passing, seemingly all at once, or in rapid secession, the There Is exercise is helpful, as well as S.E.E.I.T.

S.E.E.I.T. can help us label and differentiate what we are experiencing and encompass everything, and anything, that may come into our conscious awareness. S stands for Senses. E is for Emotion. The second E denotes Emptiness. I is the letter for Intention. And T is our Thoughts. Being able to tell the difference between one, and the other, of these mental/physical states, helps quiet the mind and bring ease and understanding to a given situation.

25

THIS WEEK

Mindful exercises to reduce stress, increase the ability to self-reflect, and learn how to live with internal and external realities. Bringing one's attention, or awareness, to the present moment with intention.

Reality of the Body and Senses
(Exercise Area—Points of Contact—page 124)

Come into the body, right where it is, in the present moment. Become aware of the touch points, the places where the body makes contact with itself, or an object. The body, and its senses, is a direct link with our state of being, and our experience of the world. The body is a barometer of emotions, thoughts and sensations. It is a rope that keeps us tethered to reality.

United In Time and Space
(Exercise Area—Be Kind—page 140)

The past has shaped us, and influenced our every action, or inaction. It can be life changing to understand why we do what we do, and discover how often what we do is due to a lack of awareness, sense of separation, and/or fear. Albert Einstein had great insight into compassion and the unifying principle of all living things. He said, "A human being is part of the whole, called by us the Universe, a part limited in time and space. He experiences himself, his thoughts and feelings, as something separate from the rest – a kind of optical delusion of his consciousness. This delusion is a kind of prison for us, restricting us to our personal desires and to affection for a few persons nearest to us. Our task must be to free ourselves from this prison by widening our circle of compassion to embrace all living creatures and the whole of nature in its beauty." It is vital to include one's self in this unifying observation.

Compassion and Kindness Begin With Awareness
(Exercise Area—There Is—page 120)

Mindfulness gives us the tools to recognize and understand our past, by acknowledging, validating, and accepting our experiences. It allows more freedom to be open to our thoughts, feelings, and emotions, regardless of their intensity or content. It is a step in developing compassion and kindness for ourselves, and others. As we develop internal awareness, and are more compassionate and gentle with our private life, we also find that we are more present to others, and have empathy and compassion for their lives and situations. We all have different circumstances, but sensations, emotions, and thoughts are universal.

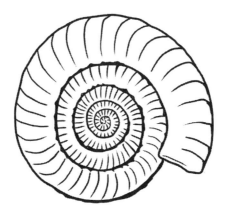

THIS WEEK

Mindful exercises to reduce stress, increase the ability to self-reflect, and learn how to live with internal and external realities. Bringing one's attention, or awareness, to the present moment with intention.

The Starting Point
(Exercise Area—There Is—page 120)

As we pursue our inner journey of mindfulness and meditation, we become more connected with our interior world and develop more understanding and compassion. We get in touch with our purpose, our passions, and what makes life meaningful. This connection with our senses, emotions and mind, is an important starting point, and a strong foundation for connecting with others more deeply and genuinely.

Connecting With the Body
(Exercise Area—Body Check—page 122)

Bringing awareness to the body helps us to identify, and be mindful of, a stressful situation, and provides a means to disentangle ourselves from typical reactions and mind traps sooner. It opens the door to new possibilities of being, and more skillful responses. The best way to foster this awareness is to continue to practice mindfulness as much as possible, and it is always possible. The very moment that you realize you aren't present; you are present once again. Connecting with the body is the key.

Observing and Differentiating Thought

(Exercise Area—P.U.F.F.—page 143)

Within, and part of, the body, is the mind. Within our mind are thoughts. The mind is always thinking, as that is its function. The brain does not say, "this thought is good" or "this thought is bad". It just thinks. Noticing our thoughts in this way can assist our understanding that what is going on internally and externally is not who we are, but what we are experiencing in the present. It is a step towards not only creating "space" between stimulus and response, but also identifying what happens in that space and giving us insight and freedom to choose.

Differentiating thoughts into categories, fields, or simplified acronyms, is one way to heighten awareness of what one is thinking, and an effective means to be mindful.

THIS WEEK

Mindful exercises to reduce stress, increase the ability to self-reflect, and learn how to live with internal and external realities. Bringing one's attention, or awareness, to the present moment with intention.

Courage and Conviction
(Exercise Area—Breath of Life—page 131)

We are not learning to simply relax, or zone out, or empty our minds, or visualize ourselves in a special, safe place, or deny that we have discomfort (with the body, emotions or thoughts). Mindful meditation takes courage and conviction, to look at, and see (internally and externally) what is taking place. We practice being awake to what is occurring, whether it is pleasant or unpleasant. Bringing attention to the breath is a good way to begin.

Being In The Present
(Exercise Area—P.U.F.F.—page 143)

Watching the breath, and being mindful, can help us quickly discover when we are getting stressed, and thus return to balance more quickly. If the day, or situation, is extremely challenging, even one minute of awareness can bring greater stillness. If we are distracted, and caught in, thoughts about the future or the past, we miss many wonderful moments in everyday life. Practice being in the present, here and now, since this is where, and when, life is lived. There is no need to try to stop thinking, or avoid our thoughts, but it can be helpful to be able to know when we are thinking, and what we are thinking about.

Being With Discomfort, Anxiety and/or Craving
(Exercise Area—Points of Contact—page 124)

Pausing, and seeing what one is thinking, can be like waking up from a dream. When we are awake, and pay attention, it is easier to lean into, and observe, what is happening, regardless of the content. Sensations, emotions and thoughts that we use to avoid, dismiss, or run away from, have less power and unconscious control of our lives. We learn to be "with" discomfort, anxiety, and craving. Instead of reacting to pain, or anger, we become a witness to its intricacies and how they come to be. When feelings or thoughts are overwhelming, or too intense, return to the body, and the points where it is touching, or being touched.

THIS WEEK

Mindful exercises to reduce stress, increase the ability to self-reflect, and learn how to live with internal and external realities. Bringing one's attention, or awareness, to the present moment with intention.

Internal Weather
(Exercise Area—Weather Report—page 145)

Take a scan of the internal weather. Notice any physical sensations, or thoughts that are arising and passing away. Are there any faint, or strong emotions? Be aware of whatever is being experienced in the moment. No need to figure it out; judge it, or try to change it. Just give it undivided attention. There may be some tension in the legs, some emotional charge over a recent incident, or thoughts about an experience, that play in the mind again and again. Instead of continuing to allow the self to identify with, and be caught in, these sensations, emotions and thoughts, step back and observe them. Give a weather report, as if you are a meteorologist looking at satellite images of clouds, storms, and changing weather patterns on a screen.

Steadfast With Full Attention
(Exercise Area—Like A Mountain—page 147)

There are times when we try to avoid what we see on the radar. If we are experiencing anxiety, or a strong gust of emotional and mental pain and confusion, we avert our attention and seek comfort, or momentary pleasure, with an object or person. By avoiding aspects of our selves, and our experience, we do not change the impact or path of painful stimulus, but only temporarily put it on hold. Whatever is happening internally, will still happen, whether we acknowledge it or not. In addition, the means or ways we use to avoid, or numb painful stimulus, may also cause additional complications and long-term consequences. Wanting is temporary. Pain is temporary. See what happens when, like a mountain, which experiences all kinds of weather, plants, and creatures, throughout the day, you remain steadfast in the body with full attention on what is taking place within.

In the Body In the Moment
(Exercise Area—Points of Contact—page 124)

Even when we are comfortable, or experiencing pleasant sensations, or thoughts, the mind tends to wants something more, something different, or something in the future, or recreate a moment from the past. We never seem to be satisfied, and continue reaching forward, or back, instead of being content with what is present. The reality is that as long as we turn away from difficult moments, and try to hold on to pleasant moments, we are captive. We are captive to habits, conditioning and craving. When we create space for the content we are experiencing, and observe what is taking place, it gives us freedom and real choice to choose and/or respond. We are also more content to be with the body, and all the points, and sensations, of contact.

THIS WEEK

Mindful exercises to reduce stress, increase the ability to self-reflect, and learn how to live with internal and external realities. Bringing one's attention, or awareness, to the present moment with intention.

Gateway to Our Being
(Exercise Area—Come To Your Senses—page 149)

If we are unaware of our emotions and thoughts, it usually corresponds with being unaware of our senses. Giving attention to the senses (sight, sound, taste, touch, smell) is a gateway to the rest of our being. It is all intricately interconnected. Like giving attention to sound, bringing awareness to any of the senses (or all of them) in the present, is a sure fire means to getting in touch with other aspects of our humanity, such as emotions, and thoughts.

Identifying Our Emotions
(Exercise Area—Emotional Sense—page151)

An old Native American tale says we have two wolves battling within us; one is mean, and the other one sweet. As to which wolf wins this battle, it depends on which one is fed. Like sensations, and thoughts, emotions are intricately connected with conditioning and habits, and do not take place in a vacuum. Our emotions are emotions. How we interpret them, or use them, can be a choice, if we are aware of them when they are occurring, and can identify what they are and how they feel.

Thinking We Are Our Thoughts
(Exercise Area—What A Thought—page 153)

Our minds wander. They are remembering the past, planning the future, or getting caught in intricate dramas in the present. We usually determine who we think we are, by these thoughts. When we bring awareness and attention to the mind, and what we are thinking, it helps us deal with unfinished business, and provides insight into how emotions and thoughts affect the body and our daily lives. Thoughts are just thoughts, but we usually associate with them as being our reality.

A Way to Remember to Remember
(Exercise Area—S.E.T.—page 155)

Learning to see, acknowledge and be with our senses, emotions and thoughts, is the road to finding freedom and choice in our lives. There is an easy way to remember to give these primary aspects of our being our attention, and that is by using the acronym S.E.T. The more awareness we bring to our bodies senses, emotions, and thoughts, the greater chance there is for them to be seen, and explored, for what they are.

THIS WEEK

Mindful exercises to reduce stress, increase the ability to self-reflect, and learn how to live with internal and external realities. Bringing one's attention, or awareness, to the present moment with intention.

Our Focus of Attention
(Exercise Area—Jelly Belly—page 206)

Our breath is always with us, and a focus of attention we can use to instantly tune into our body and mind. It is also beneficial for witnessing the ever-changing nature of life and all that comes and goes – sensations, emotions and thoughts. Belly (or diaphragmatic breathing) also calms anxiety. It is one area that is always in motion, except for the pause between breaths. Focusing on the belly, with each inhalation and exhalation, relaxes the entire nervous system.

Coming Back Into the Present
(Exercise Area—Points of Contact—page 124)

When sensations, emotions or thoughts take us into the past or future, with regret, fear, grief or anxiety, we can instantly come back to the present by focusing our attention on the body, on our physical being, at this moment, by returning our attention to our points of contact. Bringing awareness to these points of contact, or any one of them, helps remind us to be present, and be aware of what is real; our physical being.

Realizing When We Are Thinking
(Exercise Area—What a Thought—page 153)

Our minds tendency is to repeat itself, go over the past, or anticipate, plan and try to control the future. Both are helpful, in order to remember and understand, or to prepare ourselves, and arrange resources needed for living. Being caught in thought, without realizing it, can also be a means to avoid uncomfortable or stressful realities about ourselves, or our present environment. Strong, or persistent, thoughts can control our actions and beliefs, unless we give them our attention and realize when and what we are thinking.

How to Know What We Are Experiencing
(Exercise Area—S.E.T.—page 155)

Using Belly Breathing or Touch Points can bring us back into the present, and ground us in awareness of what we are experiencing, even when it is uncomfortable, stressful, or painful. Being able to distinguish between what we are experiencing internally, is just as important as it is with the external environment. Validating, and making a conscious note, of what we are aware of presently, is one way to differentiate and provide space and clarity, especially when feeling overwhelmed with sensations, emotions, or thoughts.

THIS WEEK

Mindful exercises to reduce stress, increase the ability to self-reflect, and learn how to live with internal and external realities. Bringing one's attention, or awareness, to the present moment with intention.

Living With Doubt, Anxiety and Fear
(Exercise Area—Head to Toe—page 157)

Ignoring, or trying to get rid of, doubt, anxiety, fear and tension, often leads to other reactions and behaviors we use to numb or divert ourselves from experiencing them at all. This is true for emotions and thoughts, as well as physical sensations and the senses. Bringing awareness to the body helps change these habits.

Leaning Into Our Current Condition
(Exercise Area—Come to Your Senses—page 149)

Our senses (touch, sound, sight, smell and taste) are the most direct route to learn how to lean into, and witness, our current condition. Being able to notice when we are using one sense, or another, can be a valuable tool to learn discernment, clarify our experience and bring us into the present.

When Thoughts Arise
(Exercise Area—What A Thought—page 153)

Once we can discern when we are thinking, we can learn how to further identify and label our thoughts as being about the past, the present or the future. The first step is to pay attention to our body, and the senses, and notice when a thought arises and passes away, or when we have been thinking about something.

Simple and Powerful
(Exercise Area—There Is—page 120)

What am "I" aware of right now, this minute, this second? Is it one of the senses? Is it an emotion or thought? Is it internal or external? Simple and powerful meditation begins and ends with this simple phrase, which can be applied anytime and anywhere. "There is an itch on my knee." "There is a feeling of sadness." "There is a thought." "There is…"

Investigating Our Selves
(Exercise Area—The Reporter—page 126)

Do we know we are thinking when we are thinking? More often than not, we are "caught" in our thoughts and not aware of our mind's activity; let alone what it is we are thinking about. By becoming a good investigative reporter, we are able to pause, step back, watch our mind, and the thoughts, emotions, and sensations that come and go.

THIS WEEK

Mindful exercises to reduce stress, increase the ability to self-reflect, and learn how to live with internal and external realities. Bringing one's attention, or awareness, to the present moment with intention.

What's Going On?
(Exercise Area—There Is—page 120)

What is going on? What's happening right now? What are my senses telling me about my environment and how is my internal environment (body, emotion & mind) responding? Is it sight, smell, taste, hearing or touch? What am I missing? What am I aware of? Check in with your present experience by bringing attention to the statement, "There is…" Finish the sentence with whatever comes into awareness.

Awareness Is Like the Sky
(Exercise Area—Mind in the Clouds—page 159)

Sensations are just sensations. Emotions are just emotions. Thoughts are just thoughts. They come and go. Yet, we tend to jump on board one thought after another. Where do they come from? Where do they go? What we are experiencing are like clouds in the sky. Various physical phenomena form clouds, which appear, move, change, and disappear. Awareness is the sky, and our sensations, emotions and thoughts are the clouds.

Are We Thinking Right Now?
(Exercise Area—What a Thought—page 153)

When we become aware of our thoughts, we notice that they are usually about the past, the future, or the present. Can we pay attention to our thoughts and still be here, in the moment? Do we know when we're thinking, or are we caught in our thoughts believing that is who we are at that moment? Thoughts have a powerful influence on our lives; yet we seldom know when we're thinking, let alone what we're thinking.

Consciousness Is Like the Ocean
(Exercise Area—Ocean Waves—page 161)

Each wave in the ocean is generated from other forces, moves at its own speed, eventually touches shore, and dissolves. Thoughts are similarly created from past experiences and influence our actions and reactions, but need not define who we are. If our consciousness is the ocean, then any sensations, emotions, or thoughts that are generated, that come and go, are like the waves upon the open sea.

THIS WEEK

Mindful exercises to reduce stress, increase the ability to self-reflect, and learn how to live with internal and external realities. Bringing one's attention, or awareness, to the present moment with intention.

How Time and Thoughts Define Us
(Exercise Area—Time Trip—page 163)

Can we recall the past, or predict the future? What do we remember, and how does our memory impact the present? We spend a lot of time thinking about the past, and worrying about the future. What we were thinking about a day ago, an hour ago, a minute ago, is gone. Whatever it was, is not who we are right now. What we are thinking about in the future, or think may happen, a minute from now, an hour from now, or the next day, are just thoughts. It is easy to confuse thoughts, or thinking, which we use to figure things out and plan for the future, with who we are, or with what is being experienced in the present moment.

Reliable and Present
(Exercise Area—Sound Sense—page 133)

Thoughts and feelings, whether in the past, present or future, can easily derail us from acknowledging what we are experiencing in the moment. Our senses are the most reliable, ever present, and assured way to bring us down to earth and into awareness. Bringing ones attention to any one, or all of the senses, is a reliable means of coming back to the body and seeing what is there. It is not an act of judgment, evaluation or critique, but of

42

simple and direct awareness. Sound is one of the most apparent and obvious of the senses. Giving sound our undivided attention reveals much more than one may have expected.

A Noticeable and Reliable Sensation
(Exercise Area—Jelly Belly—page 206)

When one is anxious, afraid, sad, confused, having racing thoughts and/or an agitated body, bringing attention to the senses, especially the breath, can provide immediate calm, ease and relief. As long as we are living, the breath is always with us, nourishing our body, and making it possible for us to experience sensations, emotions and thoughts. There are many points where one can notice the breath (the tip of the nose, the throat, the chest, the belly), including the complete cycle of breathing (and the pause in between). The belly can not only be felt inside, with each breath, as it rises and falls, but also by placing the hand gently over the area, and feeling it expand and contract.

THIS WEEK

Mindful exercises to reduce stress, increase the ability to self-reflect, and learn how to live with internal and external realities. Bringing one's attention, or awareness, to the present moment with intention.

A Direct Path
(Exercise Area—There Is—page 120)

Change only takes place in the present and the senses are the easiest way to come into the present. When the mind is filled with thoughts and emotions, the most direct path to being able to have space for them, and see them clearly, is by bringing awareness to the body. Any of the senses will do (sight, sound, taste, touch, smell), as we observe them shifting moment to moment.

Digging Up Dirt On Ourselves
(Exercise Area—The Reporter—page 126)

Can the mind differentiate between the senses and emotions and thoughts? Is there any space, or ability, to step back and witness what the mind is aware of at any given moment in time? By tuning into, or bringing attention repeatedly to the bodies senses, the mind can begin to see when it is thinking about the past, present or future and when it is feeling an emotion, or using one of the senses.

The Great Influencer
(Exercise Area—What A Thought—page 153)

Whether it comes from outside or inside the self, what we tell
the mind about our experience and life is what influences and/
or creates the next experience and how the mind perceives, reacts
to, and judges that experience. It is often what we tell ourselves,
that causes more suffering than the event or experience itself. Pay
attention to what you tell yourself, it can make all the difference in
the world.

From Judgment to Compassion
(Exercise Area—Be Kind—page 140)

The past influences the present, but doesn't have to define the
present, unless we are unaware of the past and continue to repeat
it by habit, circumstance and/or inattention. Once aware of
our senses, our thoughts, and what we tell ourselves about our
thoughts, there is the opportunity and freedom, to shift from
judgment to compassion for the self and others. Being kind is an
inside job, and requires honesty and understanding.

THIS WEEK

Mindful exercises to reduce stress, increase the ability to self-reflect, and learn how to live with internal and external realities. Bringing one's attention, or awareness, to the present moment with intention.

Don't Try, Just Be
(Exercise Area—Whatever—page 165)

The mind is always thinking, planning, remembering, figuring things out, or making connections. There is no need to try to stop thinking. That is what the mind is good for. With awareness, we can learn to see the changing nature of the mind and the thoughts that come and go. Wherever we are, and whatever we are doing, offers the opportunity to give it our full attention.

Putting One Number After Another
(Exercise Area—Can You Count to Ten? —page 167)

Concentration on the present helps us develop awareness and provides space to see, or witness, what is occurring. Awareness, or attention to, what we are experiencing in the moment, combined with concentration, brings more clarity to our senses, emotions and thoughts. It gives us choice and freedom from our conditioned responses. The breath brings us back to now. Breathe it all in, one breath at a time.

Constant Wonder
(Exercise Area—Points of Contact—page 124)

Bring a sense of curiosity and discovery to witnessing the internal and external world. Whatever we sense, feel or think, is actually just a flicker in the moment and not a permanent state of being. The only thing that keeps repeating itself, is the conditioning we reinforce by telling ourselves that is who we are. Practice helps us realize we are not what we experience and everything is impermanent.

Opportunity and Freedom
(Exercise Area—Be Kind—page 140)

The past influences the present, but doesn't have to define the present, unless we are unaware of the past and continue to repeat it by habit, circumstance and/or inattention. Once aware of our senses, our thoughts, and what we tell ourselves about our thoughts, there is the opportunity and freedom, to shift from judgment to compassion for the self and others. Choose to be kind to one and all (and "all" includes the self).

THIS WEEK

Mindful exercises to reduce stress, increase the ability to self-reflect, and learn how to live with internal and external realities. Bringing one's attention, or awareness, to the present moment with intention.

I Hear You Loud and Clear
(Exercise Area—Sound Sense—page 133)

When someone says, "Come to your senses," it is actually a great reminder to wake up and pay attention. Tuning into, or being aware of what we are experiencing, with any of our senses, brings us instantly into our bodies and out of our heads (for that moment). By practicing awareness of our body's senses, we can come back into the moment and have some clarity and space between what is arising and passing.

Looking In the Mirror
(Exercise Area—Face It—page 169)

Our face is like a film we project to the world. Some say the eyes are the way to the soul. Other than when looking in a mirror, we are seldom aware of how our face looks, let alone how it feels. Many of us carry, and hold, a lot of tension in the face, without realizing we are doing so. By conditioning, it is easy to unconsciously develop a permanent frown, fake smile, or a fearful, sometimes angry expression, when we are with others, let alone with ourselves. It doesn't have to stay that way.

Giving Them A Rest
(Exercise Area—Hands Down—page 171)

Our hands are usually busy "doing" something throughout the day. They help us with many tasks – eating, working, getting dressed and undressed, preparing food and driving. Even when they are "resting," they are often moving, tense or unable to stay still – tapping the leg, touching the face, cracking the knuckles, rubbing the other hand, or holding something. The hands are infrequently relaxed and at ease.

Putting It All Together
(Exercise Area—Body Check—page 122)

To connect with others, we must first connect with ourselves, and the quickest way to connect with ourselves is to bring awareness to the body. Bringing attention, with our mind, to the body (from head to toe) and taking time to focus on each area, externally and internally, relaxes the mind, and focusing the mind relaxes the body. Emotions are also connected. When the body is at ease, so are the emotions, and vice-a-versa.

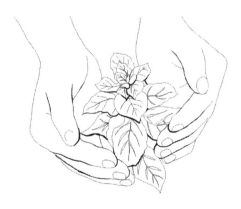

THIS WEEK

Mindful exercises to reduce stress, increase the ability to self-reflect, and learn how to live with internal and external realities. Bringing one's attention, or awareness, to the present moment with intention.

Every Breath We Take
(Exercise Area—Fresh Air—page 173)

The air we breathe gives us life every second. Focusing on the breath, and being aware of its interaction with our body, can create instant relaxation and insight. Following the breath develops concentration, quiets the mind and helps us notice what arises and passes away. The body requires a fresh supply of air with each breath. Every molecule of air that enters the body is used to full capacity, and then leaves the body to be recycled.

Cells In Sync
(Exercise Area—Inside Out—page 175)

To connect with others, connect with the self, by bringing awareness to the body. Bringing attention, with intention, to the body (from head to toe) and taking time to focus on each area, externally and internally, relaxes the mind, and focusing the mind relaxes the body. There are thousands of cells working cooperatively to keep us, and all our systems, in sync. Cells are the core and infrastructure of every organ in the body.

Neither Good or Bad
(Exercise Area—Emotional Sense—page 151)

Like the breath, and sensations in the body, emotions can build, fester, and control behavior and thoughts, without us realizing what is happening. Being able to identify an emotion as it arises, or soon after, provides some space between it and our identification with it. Emotions are transient. They come and go of their own accord. In and of themselves, emotions are neither good, nor bad, but can differ in intensity and duration.

Jumping On Board
(Exercise Area—Boxcars—page 177)

Thoughts are powerful stuff. Thinking is what our minds are programmed to do. Thinking we are our thoughts, or what we tell ourselves about our thoughts, is conditioned by our experiences, and how we react to them. Like the senses and emotions, thoughts come and go. We can have some power and choice over how we react to them, by observing them clearly, and not jumping on board, like a boxcar on a freight train, with every thought that tells a good story and captures our attention.

THIS WEEK

Mindful exercises to reduce stress, increase the ability to self-reflect, and learn how to live with internal and external realities. Bringing one's attention, or awareness, to the present moment with intention.

Pushing and Pulling
(Exercise Area—There Is—page 120)

Pushing things away, or trying to hold on, tends to dominate our daily life. We try to avoid, get rid of, or numb unpleasant sensations, emotions or thoughts, and strive to hold on to, grasp, or recreate pleasant or favorable senses, emotions and/or thoughts. Either attempt, to get rid of, or keep something present, is futile, as everything comes and goes. Instead of using our energy and time trying to recreate or forget things, focus on what is present and accept it as it is. Give it a name. Call it out. Bring it into awareness.

We Are Not What We Experience
(Exercise Area—Whatever—page 81)

Whatever comes up and passes away, with our minds, emotions and senses, can be witnessed and seen for what it is, as opposed to diving into each with our attention and letting it sweep us away. It is easy for one to believe that we are what we are experiencing or thinking, as opposed to what we are witnessing and experiencing is a temporary phenomenon and not a self-defining event. Shift from resignation of "Whatever," to "Whatever comes my way!"

Let the Body Be Your Guide
(Exercise Area—Space - The Final Frontier—page 184)

When the body is in a relaxed state, and aware of the senses and areas of tension or tightness, the emotions and mind tend to also relax, making it easier to observe what is arising and passing away, without getting caught in it. When the mind is aware and concentrated on the present moment, it helps the body and emotions to settle. We can "be with" the experiences that we notice second to second, as opposed to trying to control them. Letting the body relax, is often easier said than done. Here's one way.

Coming back to the Center
(Exercise Area—Jelly Belly—page 206)

If the mind is racing, or the body is extremely agitated, or anxious, tuning into the breath can bring us back to earth. Noticing the parts of the body that rise and fall with each breath benefits all aspects of our being. One can focus on the chest, as it rises and falls, or on the belly, as it extends and contracts with each breath. When the belly is relaxed, the rest of the body follows, including the mind.

THIS WEEK

Mindful exercises to reduce stress, increase the ability to self-reflect, and learn how to live with internal and external realities. Bringing one's attention, or awareness, to the present moment with intention.

The Senses Are the Remedy
(Exercise Area—There Is—page 120)

There is so much we miss day-to-day, let alone moment-to-moment. We seldom pay attention to what is coming into awareness, or what just happened. Everything is on automatic. Our responses and perceptions to external and internal stimuli, and our process of how we react to, and perceive them, is rarely noticed, let alone identified and understood. The remedy begins with the senses and giving a shout out to what is there.

All Lumped Together
(Exercise Area—S.E.T.—page 155)

In addition to the five senses, emotions and thoughts tend to dominate our waking lives. They come and go, pulling us this way and that. We lump them together – believing we are what we are feeling or thinking in the moment. Like our senses, it can make a world of difference when we pause, sit back, and take an honest look at what we are feeling and thinking. Differentiating one aspect of our experience from another is enlightening.

Five Qualities of Being
(Exercise Area—S.E.E.I.T.—page 135)

In addition to the senses, emotions and thoughts, there are also times we are conscious of emptiness and intention. Emptiness has a different quality to it than depression or feeling alone. Emptiness is simply a moment when we are unaware of any senses, emotions, thoughts or other states of consciousness being present. Intentions are what we plan to do, or create, or have happen. It is advantages to differentiate between senses, emotions, emptiness, and thoughts, and look at our deepest intentions, with complete candor.

All Desire Is Temporary
(Exercise Area—S.E.E.D.I.T.—page 181)

Desire is a form of energy that can be directed towards anything or anyone. Don't deny it, try to hold on to it, or push it away. Observe it. Like all other experiences of the senses, emotions, emptiness, intentions, and thoughts, desire is temporary. The time and energy we use to fulfill a desire, is created by how much attention and belief we have in it making us happy, or feeling good (if even for a minute). Ultimately, it is temporary.

THIS WEEK

Mindful exercises to reduce stress, increase the ability to self-reflect, and learn how to live with internal and external realities. Bringing one's attention, or awareness, to the present moment with intention.

Rising and Falling
(Exercise Area—Jelly Belly—page 206)

With every breath, the belly rises and falls. If it is moving rapidly, it may be a sign of anxiety or exertion. If it is barely moving, one may be tense, or not breathing fully. A relaxed, gentle rising and falling of the belly can help the body to relax, the emotions to settle, and the mind to quiet itself. Becoming aware of the belly with each breath grounds us in the moment. Let it be and lighten up.

Everything Takes Place Within It
(Exercise Area—Space - The Final Frontier—page 184)

We are often caught in, and concentrate on, emotions, thoughts, places, people, events and objects. Awareness of the space that precedes, encompasses and surrounds our experience, is hardly noticed, utilized, or validated. Yet, it is within these spaces that everything takes place and has its being. There is a pause after each breath. We move and have our being in space. Our bodies are a small form within infinite space.

Touching Base
(Exercise Area—Points of Contact—page 124)

Coming "back to earth", "getting grounded", "touching base", are all useful phrases for remembering the body within which we live, and usually have little contact or awareness of. We are constantly surrounded by buildings, nature, other people and objects, yet there are always parts of our human form that are touching and being touched. Focusing awareness on these areas can anchor us back into the present.

Every Step of the Way
(Exercise Area—The Urge—page 187)

Desire encompasses more than sex or food. It is with us every step of the way, and every step of the day. Wanting the moment to be different than it is, trying to hold on to something from the past, or craving something in the future, are all aspects of desire, or wanting. Desire keeps us alive, but awareness of our desires (urges), as they unfold, can provide much more freedom and choice. Watch desire, acknowledge it, and let it be.

THIS WEEK

Mindful exercises to reduce stress, increase the ability to self-reflect, and learn how to live with internal and external realities. Bringing one's attention, or awareness, to the present moment with intention.

An Internal Microscope
(Exercise Area—Come to Your Senses—page 149)

Feeling pain is a natural reaction to painful stimulus. The pain can be physical, emotional, and/or mental. Pain is part of life and living. Suffering is what we add on to pain, by what we tell ourselves when, and after, we have experienced something painful. We cannot avoid pain, but we can learn how to not add additional pain and suffering by honestly acknowledging what is present. Use awareness to investigate sensations in the body, like an internal microscope.

An Intricate Part of Living
(Exercise Area—Good Grief—page 188)

Everything and everyone dies, moves on, changes course, and/or goes away. There is no relationship with another being, or with any kind of matter, that stays the same and is permanent. Loss is an intricate part of living. We lose people to death. We lose friends, jobs, homes, expectations, and material objects. Do we recognize and acknowledge our losses? Do we let ourselves grieve a loss, push it away or try to forget about it? When we experience a loss, be B.R.A.V.E. Before Reacting Access Validate and Explore.

58

Diving Into Desire
(Exercise Area—The Urge—page 187

Some of us dive into desire and follow one urge after
another, unaware, and unconscious of, its affects or long-term
consequences. At other times, we avoid, or try to push away,
desire, in an effort to not get caught or distracted from other life
tasks. An urge for something, or someone, is part of reality, as is
wanting a moment to be different. There is no need to jump in, or
run away from desire. Take the opportunity to see it, name it and
realize you are not it, but experiencing it. Believe it or not, desire
is temporary.

Coming Back Home
(Exercise Area—The Old One Two—page 190)

Come back to the home that is always with us – our human
form. Come back to the body – back to the breath. Breathe
in. Breathe out. Take one breath at a time. Being aware of the
breath, is a true-blue way to bring oneself into the present – the
here and now. As simple as it may sound, counting the breath
with each inhale and exhale is a powerful means to developing
concentration, and giving attention to what is presently your
reality.

THIS WEEK

Mindful exercises to reduce stress, increase the ability to self-reflect, and learn how to live with internal and external realities. Bringing one's attention, or awareness, to the present moment with intention.

Wherever We Go
(Exercise Area—The Old One Two—page 190)

Breathing happens, whether we are aware of it or not. When we pay attention to our breath, it brings us immediately into the body, the senses, and the present moment. Wherever we go, and whatever we do, includes breathing – precious air entering and leaving the body. Being able to concentrate on the breath, one at a time, improves concentration, and makes it easier to practice awareness.

I Want That
(Exercise Area—The Urge—page 187)

What's wrong with this moment? Why do we wish it to be otherwise? Where do we think we need to go? What do we believe we need to do? What takes us on one mindless and emotional journey after another? It is desire and wanting. We constantly want this moment to be different - to obtain something; change something; create something. Can there be peace and satisfaction in the here and now, without following our desires?

Avoidance Is Costly
(Exercise Area—I Don't Like That—page 192)

We rarely notice how much of our lives we live trying to get rid of something or someone; trying to avoid, control or manipulate a situation in order to avoid it or push it away. Aversion has deep affects and can keep one endlessly avoiding, and thus often missing, other realities and experiences that are occurring in the present. Disliking things, or people, leaves little room for gratitude, or appreciation of what is.

You're No Good
(Exercise Area—Enough Already—page 194)

"I'm not enough." "I'm no good." "I'm helpless, useless, unlovable, ugly, stupid, blah blah blah." People, cultures, families, and friends, often reinforce these feelings and beliefs, that we are not enough. To top it off, we start to believe it, and tell ourselves the same thing over and over and over. Noticing our senses, emotions and thoughts, can give us some space to witness such conditioning. Seeing it clearly is what helps it change. By shedding a spotlight of awareness on such thoughts, we can let them be, and let them go.

THIS WEEK

Mindful exercises to reduce stress, increase the ability to self-reflect, and learn how to live with internal and external realities. Bringing one's attention, or awareness, to the present moment with intention.

Nothing Is Set In Concrete
(Exercise Area—Space – The Final Frontier—page 184)

Our habits, conditioning and automatic reactions to life, do not need to continue; but unless we know how to stop, hit the pause button, and observe what is going on, they will. We are always affected by our environment and other people - past, present and future. Those affects do not need to become embedded in our lives like concrete. Pause, take a breath, slow down and see what is going on.

Spinning Out of Control
(Exercise Area—S.E.T.—page 155)

Learning to differentiate our experiences with senses, emotions, and thoughts, decreases feelings of being overwhelmed or spinning out of control. To be able to decipher, and see, the exact moment we are aware of one of the senses, an emotion, and/or a thought, helps us break out of the self-imposed trance, which we often call life, but is often unconscious and recycled habits we use for survival. Break up these habits into S.E.T. When they are not all huddled together, they come out into the open.

Accepting Ourselves As Is
(Exercise Area—Enough Already—page 194)

Is this moment ever enough? Is this one breath, right now, all we need? Do we think we are enough; have enough; are good enough? We seldom see, or witness, the sensations, emotions and thoughts that are arising and passing away, let alone accept them as they are. Even more poignant, are the thoughts we have about our experiences, and the judgments we feed ourselves about who we think we are, or believe we are.

Like A Satellite
(Exercise Area—Weather Report—page 145)

Meeting every moment with an open heart and mind takes courage and tenacity. It's not always pleasant, or easy, and is usually a mixed bag of pain, pleasure, sadness, joy, shame, happiness, anger, frustration, aversion and clarity. Be like a satellite and say, "Yes" to whatever comes into your sphere, by acknowledging its presence. Saying, "Yes" doesn't mean we like it or agree with it, but we see it, and don't deny its existence.

THIS WEEK

Mindful exercises to reduce stress, increase the ability to self-reflect, and learn how to live with internal and external realities. Bringing one's attention, or awareness, to the present moment with intention.

Pleasant Or Unpleasant
(Exercise Area—There Is—page 120)

What we identify with is what we perpetuate. What we think of as "me", or "I", or "self", is only a momentary attachment with the senses, emotions and/or thoughts. In order to see clearly, and discover who we are (or aren't), look closely at what is present, and acknowledge the experience in the moment, regardless of its content, and whether it is pleasant or unpleasant. Pay attention. Take notice. Be aware.

Everything We Do
(Exercise Area—S.E.T.—page 155)

Difficult emotions, and thoughts, are uncomfortable and can create tension in the body. When we are not watching closely, and unconscious of something that is "bothering" us, or feeling "bad," it gets stored in the body and mind and affects everything we do. Bringing attention, and awareness to a painful, or difficult emotion or thought, helps relax the body and mind. Separate what is going on, and give it a name.

It's All In Your Head
(Exercise Area—Face It—page 169)

The head of the body holds the mind and all the senses. It is the control center that's open 24 hours a day. The head also contains hundreds of muscles, bones, blood vessels, and nerves; and the ears, mouth, nose, tongue, and eyes. Tension in our face, around the jaw, mouth, temples, forehead and eyes, can be lessened, with close attention and care. It appears, that every part of the body affects the rest of the body. Relax that noggin.

Hokusai Says by Roger Keyes

Hokusai says look carefully. He says pay attention, notice. He says keep looking, stay curious. He says there is no end to seeing. He says everything is alive – shells, buildings, people, fish, mountains, trees. Wood is alive. Water is alive. Everything has its own life. Everything lives inside us. He says live with the world inside you. It matters that you care. It matters that you feel. It matters that you notice. It matters that life lives through you. Look, feel; let life take you by the hand. Let life live through you.

THIS WEEK

Mindful exercises to reduce stress, increase the ability to self-reflect, and learn how to live with internal and external realities. Bringing one's attention, or awareness, to the present moment with intention.

Immediate and Real
(Exercise Area—Sound Sense—page 133)

The senses are immediate and real, at least as real as real can be. They are the means by which we experience life and everything it offers. By tuning into the senses, or a single sense, we can discover what is present in the present. Awareness of a sense helps us tune into the here and now and plant our feet in the ground (literally & figuratively). Sound is often the first sense that we are aware of. Listen for external and internal sounds.

I Want That
(Exercise Area—Your Heart's Desire—page 196)

I want this. I want that. I have everything I want and I want something more; something different; something else. What is the nature of wanting? What do we desire most? Underneath the endless wanting and desire for the moment, situation, environment or people to be different, what does our heart crave most deeply? Is there something at the core of our heart's desire? What do we really want?

Cutting Through Conditioning
(Exercise Area—S.T.O.P.—page 127)

"Hurry up." "Get over here." "Get out of here." "Get it together." "Eat, walk, run, talk, and work." "Keep moving." "Keep going over future plans, so everything works out and you have control over what happens." "Think about the past and try to figure out what happened; who to blame; what went wrong." These are the messages we constantly receive from others and what we tell ourselves. S.T.O.P.

Care and Compassion
(Exercise Area—Be Kind—page 140)

Within the space that we have our being, and in which our bodies abide, there is an endless supply of care and compassion for ourselves and others, if we become aware of our judging mind and allow kindness to come in and out with each breath. Compassion resides within our fear, pain and suffering. In spite of our conditioning or history, kindness and care are always accessible.

THIS WEEK

Mindful exercises to reduce stress, increase the ability to self-reflect, and learn how to live with internal and external realities. Bringing one's attention, or awareness, to the present moment with intention.

Getting Unstuck
(Exercise Area—There Is—page 120)

When you pause, take a breath and observe, what is there? When the breath, body and mind have slowed down, and we pay attention to our senses, feelings and thoughts, what do we experience? What is within our awareness? Are the sensations, emotions or thoughts permanent and solid, or do they come and go? Do we get "stuck" in a train of thought, and sucked into a long drama? What the frack is going on?

Reality Check
(Exercise Area—B.R.A.V.E.—page 198)

Let's get real and be B.R.A.V.E., if only for a few minutes of our lives. We don't have to know everything, figure it all out, or understand what is going on. Just choose to pause, observe, and honestly acknowledge whatever we are experiencing in the moment. Recognize what is taking place, without reacting. Acknowledge what is present. Explore and investigate it is as a witness, not a subject.

Traps and Sieves
(Exercise Area—What A Thought—page 153)

Our minds are like traps and sieves, often at the same time. Some thoughts seem to not be able to get away and others come and go, like small fish in a big porous net. Where do they come from? Where do they go? What triggers one thought to lead to another? Can we control our thoughts, make the one's we don't like go away, and hold on to the ones we like? Thoughts are just thoughts, even though we think they are everything.

Safe Harbor
(Exercise Area—Body Anchor—page 200)

No matter where we go, or what we do, our bodies are always with us. As long as we live and breathe, the body and its senses can bring us to a safe harbor. By paying attention to the breath, focusing on one of the senses, or scanning the body and its organs, for tension, unease or tightness, we can quiet our thoughts, relax, and remember the core of our being. When the sea of life is stormy, drop anchor by focusing on the body.

THIS WEEK

Mindful exercises to reduce stress, increase the ability to self-reflect, and learn how to live with internal and external realities. Bringing one's attention, or awareness, to the present moment with intention.

Settling the Mind With the Gut
(Exercise Area—Jelly Belly—page 206)

Air not only enters the body through the nose, down the throat and into the lungs, it also causes the belly to rise and fall. Bringing awareness to the belly, and noticing any discomfort, or tightness it may hold, releases physical and emotional tension. The belly is working throughout the day, helping with digestion, and absorbing nutrients. Relaxing the belly, with each breath, settles the mind.

Concentration and Mindfulness
(Exercise Area—Head To Toe—page 157)

To be able to pay attention to our mind and emotions, it is helpful to also develop concentration and attentiveness. By focusing on a specific area in the body, or an external object, we strengthen our ability to see what comes and goes, without getting as distracted and pulled into drama and temporary phenomena. Concentration goes hand in hand with mindfulness and is the foundation for insight.

Like A Computer
(Exercise Area—What A Thought—page 153)

The mind is like a computer that is never turned off and has no controls. It works by memory and conditioning, and makes connections, assumptions, judgments and thoughts based on our past and present stimulus and experience. If we don't occasionally watch our thoughts, our lives are pre-programmed. Observing the mind, as opposed to jumping on board each thought, is like turning on a light to see in the dark.

Jumping Like A Grasshopper
(Exercise Area—Points of Contact—page 124)

If the mind is jumping around like grasshoppers, and our emotions are leaking like a bucket with a large hole in it, we can always touch base with our body and find the points that are making physical contact with one another, or other objects in our world. We don't need to control thoughts or emotions in order to do this. We just need to remember to do it. Parts of our body are always making contact.

THIS WEEK

Mindful exercises to reduce stress, increase the ability to self-reflect, and learn how to live with internal and external realities. Bringing one's attention, or awareness, to the present moment with intention.

From Without and From Within
(Exercise Area—Sound Sense—page 133)

There are many sounds we hear throughout the day. Some sounds come from without, and some from within. At times, it all seems like a bunch of noise. At other times, it is specific. Sometimes it is directed at us when someone is speaking. Most of the time, our ears are physically hearing, but we are seldom listening. Listen closely. Sound is just sound. Our minds interpret and give it meaning.

Touching Base
(Exercise Area—Come to Your Senses—page 149)

Where do sound, sight and speech come from? Are we aware of the process by which we experience these senses? Is there any way to pay attention to what is actually taking place in the moment with these stimuli? More importantly, where do speech, sound and sight begin? Are we seeing, hearing and speaking internally, before it reaches our mouth, ears or eyes? Let the senses be a guide to touch base, and be present.

Life's Play
(Exercise Area—The Reporter—page 126)

Instead of being actors in life's play, and automatically repeating what we are told, believe, or conditioned ourselves to do; we can become the writers, directors, and producers, and choose which parts we wish to play. In order to do this, we must become good reporters – gaining access to what is happening, and honestly making note of everything we see and experience – What? Who? When? Where? Why? How?

Solid As Stone
(Exercise Area—Like A Mountain—page 147)

Mountains are immovable. Mountains are solid. Mountains go through thousands of years of life, death, and transformation. Mountains are not moved, or swayed by one season over another. They remain mountains regardless of the external or internal stimulus. When we are able to observe our senses, emotions and thoughts, and not get caught in them, we are like mountains.

THIS WEEK

Mindful exercises to reduce stress, increase the ability to self-reflect, and learn how to live with internal and external realities. Bringing one's attention, or awareness, to the present moment with intention.

Direct Contact
(Exercise Area—Come To Your Senses—page 149)

There are many ways to "come to your senses" and get in touch with the body. One of the quickest, and most convenient, is to bring awareness to one of the five senses (taste, touch, sight, hearing, speaking) and bring attention to how that sense is being experienced in the present moment. The body, and its senses, is how we live in the world. It is how we make direct contact with ourselves and the environment.

Fingers and Hands
(Exercise Area—Hands Down—page 171)

Our hands and fingers are such a vital part of our daily life, but are rarely noticed, unless we lose some, or one or more are incapacitated because of an injury. They are used to hold things, shake someone's hand, provide comfort and care, grasp tools and material objects for work, recreation or play, and for expressing one's self. Instead of focusing on the entire body, use the following exercise with just the fingers and hands.

When Things Feel Like A Mess
(Exercise Area—S.E.T.—page 155)

Sometimes, everything feels like a mess. A pain in our back is
constant. Sadness about something that we did pulls relentlessly
at our hearts. The chatter in our mind takes on one imaginary
scenario after another. Mix them all together and it can feel
overwhelming. Learning to differentiate between our senses,
emotions and thoughts, is like being thrown a life preserver when
we are drowning, or learning how to swim.

The Umbilical Cord
(Exercise Area—Jelly Belly—page 206)

It's been with us since birth - a physical reminder of the
connection to our mother. The naval (bellybutton) was our lifeline
for all sustenance before we were born and became air breathers.
We would not have survived without the umbilical cord. Yet,
when that cord was cut, it did not severe our interdependence
and connection with others, and the environment, to live. The
bellybutton is humanity's common thread.

THIS WEEK

Mindful exercises to reduce stress, increase the ability to self-reflect, and learn how to live with internal and external realities. Bringing one's attention, or awareness, to the present moment with intention.

Your Attention Please
(Exercise Area—Come To Your Senses—page 149)

When one is in the military, the command "Come to attention!" means to stand up straight and bring complete focus to the moment, and the officer who said it. Without being tense and physically standing, it is possible to bring awareness into the present and give our senses and inner world the same kind of attention, as if we had been commanded to "Come to our senses!"

I've Got Your Back
(Exercise Area—Body Check—page 122)

"Put your back into it." "Sit up straight." "Use a little backbone." These are all familiar phrases that convey the importance of the spine, not only for strength, but also to stand and sit, and hold up our heads. The spine, and its bones (vertebrae), is a core part of our body and how we move and have our being in the world. Check in daily with the spine, and the rest of the body.

Always Thinking
(Exercise Area—There Is—page 120)

Once we are paying attention to the world within (and without),
aware of our posture, and any tension or tightness that we are
holding in the body, we can also bring our awareness to the mind
and notice when we are, or are not, thinking. The mind is always
thinking, but we are not always aware of what those thoughts are,
let alone what they are conveying, and how we are interpreting
them.

Running On Automatic
(Exercise Area—S.E.E.I.T.—page 135)

Our thoughts often run on automatic, without any self-awareness,
as do countless other aspects of life. Noticing when we are having
an emotion, or having a physical sensation, are just as vital as
awareness of thoughts. Emptiness and intention are additional
and common phenomena. Emptiness can feel detached, or
unemotional. Intention is a momentary, or long held desire or
wish, for something, or someone, to be a certain way.

THIS WEEK

Mindful exercises to reduce stress, increase the ability to self-reflect, and learn how to live with internal and external realities. Bringing one's attention, or awareness, to the present moment with intention.

Let's Get Personal
(Exercise Area—Body Check—page 122)

How well do we know or understand, what is happening with our senses and the body within which they reside? Do we ever pay attention to the tension, discomfort, or changes taking place each day, each hour, each minute? Let's get personal, and intimate, and take a good look at our body – from head to toe (or vice-a-versa). Focusing on the body reduces stress and increases awareness.

The Respirator
(Exercise Area—The Old One Two—page 190)

Our bodies are one big respirator. They take in good air, use the oxygen provided to all the organs that need it, and discard the used air to be recycled and used again. The breath is always coming and going. When it enters the body, the chest expands and the belly extends. When it leaves the body, the chest and stomach relax. Like an accordion, we continue to breathe in and breathe out the music of life.

Being The Observer
(Exercise Area—S.E.T.—page 155)

Identifying a given state of mind, or experience, as an observer
and not solely as participant, provides space and choice. When we
are not caught in our thoughts (about the past, present, or future),
or our emotions, or senses, we create a moment of freedom.
Differentiating between the senses, emotions and thoughts, is
one means of bringing these experiences into our awareness and
having a choice how to respond.

The Four Seasons of Thought
(Exercise Area—P.U.F.F.—page 143)

We all have difficult moments, situations, and experiences. Instead
of trying to avoid thoughts about the past, present, or future, let's
look them "in the face" and see what happens. Instead of running
away, shutting out, or trying to avoid unpleasant, or painful,
thoughts, let's bring them to mind and observe them closely. Do
they define us, or are we able to define them as living in the past,
unfolding, a fantasy or the future?

THIS WEEK

Mindful exercises to reduce stress, increase the ability to self-reflect, and learn how to live with internal and external realities. Bringing one's attention, or awareness, to the present moment with intention.

Storms On The Horizon
(Exercise Area—Weather Report—page 145)

There are internal storms, hurricanes, sunshine, rain, wind, turbulence, rainbows, clouds, floods, and other combinations of weather, taking place within the body and mind. At times, it seems as if there are lulls and at others it is as if the downpour will never end. Just like weather, sensations, emotions and thoughts come and go. Some are stronger, or more intense than others, and some are subtle and below the radar.

Villain, Hero and Victim
(Exercise Area—B.R.A.V.E.—page 198)

Pay close attention to yourself and others. Are there specific personality traits that you notice or are aware of? If you observe closely, you will find that we tend to alternate between three dominant characters, or traits. They are not good or bad traits, just ones we have used to adapt to our lives, and repeat unconsciously. We have them all, and switch from one to the other, but tend to have one prominent type over another.

These traits are Villain, Hero and Victim. We play them out without being aware of what we are doing, or the drama we perpetuate. The Villain personality tends to believe that, "I'm no good." "I'm bad." "Nobody's going to tell me what to do." "I'll show them!" "I'm worthless." The Hero tells themselves that, "I'm here to save you and protect you." "I'm in control." "I know what's right and wrong." "I'm in control." The Victim says, "I'm helpless." "Why me?" "It's always the same." "It never works out." Use B.R.A.V.E. to recognize your dominant trait.

It's A Choice
(Exercise Area—Be Kind—page 140)

Some people are difficult to be with, or around. Others are difficult for us at specific times, or about specific things. Our behavior, or attitude, may be annoying to others as well. Words and actions may, or may not (usually they don't), change the situation or person who appears to be bugging you. We do have a choice in how we react, but must first look honestly at ourselves. The choice in how we respond can always be with kindness.

THIS WEEK

Mindful exercises to reduce stress, increase the ability to self-reflect, and learn how to live with internal and external realities. Bringing one's attention, or awareness, to the present moment with intention.

Where Was I?
(Exercise Area—Can You Count to Ten? —page 167)

It seems simple. Count from one to ten without your mind wandering, or losing track of which number you're on. One, two, three, four... "Where was I?" "What was I thinking about?" "Damn, I lost count again." Concentration, in and of itself, is beneficial to our health and wellbeing. When combined with awareness, it can also be a catalyst for personal growth and insight.

All Stirred Up
(Exercise Area—What A Thought—page 153)

"They really piss me off." "Why did they do that?" "What were they thinking?" "I'm stupid." "Everything I do turns out badly." "It's hopeless. I'll never change." These kinds of thoughts and feelings come and go, but we increase the pain by adding additional thoughts of blame, guilt, and helplessness. We stir them up, or wallow in them, without realizing that we are not only throwing poison at others, but also drinking it ourselves.

Just Sit
(Exercise Area—Whatever—page 165)

If we just sit for five to ten minutes, without any goal, or specific intention, what happens? Without paying attention, or being aware, of our senses, emotions and thoughts during that time, we often miss out on the present moment and being fully awake to life as it is unfolding. Just sitting, and consciously observing what takes place, can be an eye-opening experience, without opening the eyes.

We All Suffer
(Exercise Area—Good Grief—page 188)

Nobody is immune to suffering, yet we often believe that we are the only person who has ever experiencing the pain or discomfort we are experiencing at the moment. Whether it is physical, emotional, and/or mental; we can feel isolated and alone with our own perceptions. Yet, at any given time, there are thousands of people experiencing similar suffering. Grief and loss seem to be intricately mixed with love and attachment.

THIS WEEK

Mindful exercises to reduce stress, increase the ability to self-reflect, and learn how to live with internal and external realities. Bringing one's attention, or awareness, to the present moment with intention.

Wake Up
(Exercise Area—The Old One Two—page 190)

One two, buckle my shoe. Waking up and being aware of life is as simple as counting one and two. Being simple however, does not mean that it is easy. To refocus our attention on the breath, and remember to do so, moment to moment, takes continued intention, attention and practice. By focusing on the breath, we come into the body, and by coming into the body we come into the inner realms of emotion and thought.

The Gift Of Thought
(Exercise Area—P.U.F.F.—page 143)

There are so few moments that we are truly present. Let's have some of those moments be now. This moment is a gift. Can we see it, feel it, think it, or rather observe ourselves doing so, and be truly awake? Paying attention to this moment is an inviting opportunity to receive one present after another. That thought was the past. That one is the future. That one is fantasy. Look, here's the present. What a wonderful gift.

Winds Of Change
(Exercise Area—Weather Report—page 145)

Acknowledging, observing and being a witness to what we are aware of, without trying to distort it, push it away, or hold on to it, is a true act of acceptance. Saying yes to what is present, regardless of the content or experience, can be difficult. Saying, "Yes" does not mean we like or dislike what comes into awareness, but that we are willing to look at it honestly. Use the inner radar to see what's up, or down, or spinning around.

We All Hurt
(Exercise Area—Good Grief—page 188)

Nobody is immune to suffering. In fact, its presence is one of the ways in which we are all connected and inter-related. Suffering is suffering. What we tell ourselves about suffering can either add on more suffering, or lesson its impact. No need to pour salt on a wound. Remembering that we all have pain, hardships, illness, and loss, can awaken our compassion for ourselves and others.

THIS WEEK

Mindful exercises to reduce stress, increase the ability to self-reflect, and learn how to live with internal and external realities. Bringing one's attention, or awareness, to the present moment with intention.

The Body Doesn't Lie
(Exercise Area—Points Of Contact—page 124)

The body doesn't lie. It tells us what we need to know and when we need to know it. Being aware of our body and its senses, reminds us where we are and what is going on. Focusing on where our body is touching something, or being touched, is one of the ways we can remember to tune in and pay attention to what is happening in the present. Any of the points will do, or shifting attention from one to the other.

Acronyms and Abbreviations
(Exercise Area—B.R.A.V.E.—page 198)

There are a lot of acronyms and abbreviations in language that are created to help remember and simplify concepts. B.R.A.V.E is one acronym, or mnemonic, that describes one of the processes that can be utilized for mindful meditation. It is a reminder that before reacting to any internal or external stimuli we can access what is taking place, validate or acknowledge what it is, and explore it for greater understanding.

We Are What We Seek
(Exercise Area—Enough Already—page 194)

Is there ever enough? Are we ever enough? Are we always lacking? Is there something missing? Or, are we, and what we are experiencing in the moment, perfect for that moment? Is what we identify as "me" or "I" simply a compilation of previous conditioning and habits: some which we have enabled, and others, which are imposed? What if "we" are complete already? What if now is enough?

Desire After Desire
(Exercise Area—The Urge—page 187)

"It's got me mad and won't let go." "There's a monkey on my back." "I've got to have this, or that over there." "I will not be happy until this desire is fulfilled." "I will not be happy until this present situation changes." "I will not be satisfied until they change or act like I want them too." Desire after desire; one urge after another. They seem to be endless, because they are. How do we live with desire?

THIS WEEK

Mindful exercises to reduce stress, increase the ability to self-reflect, and learn how to live with internal and external realities. Bringing one's attention, or awareness, to the present moment with intention.

Self-Imposed Lockdown
(Exercise Area—Whatever—page 165)

Though we do it often, it seems to be impossible to completely lock down our feelings, emotions and thoughts. No matter what situation we are in, how many drugs or how much alcohol we've used, the mind and emotions still work full time and in full force. Perhaps instead of trying to numb out, or lockdown these experiences, we should just sit awhile, and give whatever comes up our attention.

There's Thinking and There Is Thinking
(Exercise Area—There Is—page 120)

Thinking and thinking about thinking, are one and the same. But, when are we thinking, or having a different experience, such as a sensation, using one of the senses, or feeling an emotion? By bringing awareness and concentration to the body we begin to decipher when we are caught in thoughts, or simply aware of what, or if, we are thinking. There is always something going on, might as well know what it is.

Everything Changes
(Exercise Area—S.E.T.—page 155)

Nothing is set in stone. Everything changes – some faster than others. Even stones change over time. The same is true for the senses, emotions and thoughts, which come and go in our daily lives. An emotion can spark a memory, or thought. A sensation can elicit an emotion. They are often so mixed up and/or change so fast, that we are seldom aware of them at the moment, let alone differentiate one from the other.

Hello and Goodbye
(Exercise Area—P.U.F.F.—page 143)

All we know comes and goes. How often do we greet them as they arrive, and say goodbye, as they go? Our thoughts also come and go. Usually we don't realize, or recognize, one from the other until they are already with us or have already left. Say hello to each thought, as soon as you are aware of it, and goodbye, as it fades away. Begin to see whether it is the past, unfolding in the present, a fantasy, or about the future.

THIS WEEK

Mindful exercises to reduce stress, increase the ability to self-reflect, and learn how to live with internal and external realities. Bringing one's attention, or awareness, to the present moment with intention.

Nothing To Do
(Exercise Area—The Old One Two—page 190)

There is nothing to do at this moment, other than breathe. Watch the breath as it comes and goes; as it enters the body and leaves; as it fills the lungs and departs. Whenever you find your mind wandering or caught in some past, present or future drama or memory, bring it back to the breath. Breathe in. Breathe out. The mind is always thinking, and the breath is always moving. Come back to the breath.

Coming and Going
(Exercise Area—There Is—page 120)

What is going on right now, this minute; this second? What are you experiencing as you hear or read these words? What are you aware of? Is it one of the senses of hearing, sensation, speaking, listening or tasting? Is it an emotion? Is it a thought? Is there a combination of feelings, thoughts and sensations? Pay attention and see what is arising here and now at this time and this place.

Before We Die
(Exercise Area—Good Grief—page 188)

Life is short. People say that all the time, especially when looking at the brief span of our lives. Some decide that they do not want to spend the rest of their lives caught in endless strife, desire, or negative activities. Many times, when we have experienced a major loss, or someone we know has, it wakes us up to the preciousness of life. Let us wake up now, before we die, or something traumatic takes place.

If You Die Tomorrow
(Exercise Area—The Casket—page 202)

Do you know when you will die or how long you will live? If you died tomorrow, and you looked back on your life, what would you see? What would stand out? If there is anything you could change, what would it be? What is your life about? What would you say about yourself at your own funeral if yesterday had been your last day alive? Every life matters, including yours. Start acting like it.

THIS WEEK

Mindful exercises to reduce stress, increase the ability to self-reflect, and learn how to live with internal and external realities. Bringing one's attention, or awareness, to the present moment with intention.

Day Or Night
(Exercise Area—S.T.O.P.—page 127)

Anywhere, anytime of the day or night, pause and tell yourself to stop. Stop what you are doing, take a breath, observe what is happening (internally and externally), and then proceed with awareness. Every time we remember to stop, or pause, we have the opportunity to notice our breath, see what we are feeling, thinking or sensing, and choose how to continue, change and S.T.O.P. again.

System By System
(Exercise Area—Beam Me Up Scotty—page 184)

We hold everything in our body. The body is like an automobile or computer, yet more complicated. If we tune in, listen, watch for clues, actions and reactions, we can tell when and where it needs attention, maintenance or a complete overhaul. Going system by system, from head to toe, allows us to discover where there is tension, tightness or unease. Each area of the body is unique, yet connected.

Something More
(Exercise Area—Inquiring Mind—page 138)

Have you ever asked yourself who you are or taken a close look at who you "think" you are? Are we just a body? Are we an array of thoughts? Does what we are feeling, or thinking in the moment, define us? Is there something more? Are we honest about what we see, when we look at ourselves? Do we believe we are what other people, society, culture, or religion tells us we are? Who am I, really?

Let It Be
(Exercise Area—Whatever—page 165)

Years ago, some famous lads in England wrote a song called "Let It Be." The lyrics included, "when the broken hearted people, living in the world agree, there will be an answer, let it be." We rarely allow ourselves to let anything be, let alone our constant grasping, planning, or trying to fix things. When we let things be, just for a millisecond, it opens the door and window to awareness, and nourishes contentment, acceptance and momentary peace.

THIS WEEK

Mindful exercises to reduce stress, increase the ability to self-reflect, and learn how to live with internal and external realities. Bringing one's attention, or awareness, to the present moment with intention.

Mindful Meditation
(Exercise Area—Can You Count to Ten? —page 167)

Mindful meditation isn't some esoteric dream state, or attempt to be in bliss and reach cosmic consciousness; though some meditation practices try to do so. With mindful meditation, we aren't trying to escape, or get away from ourselves, but look closely at who we are, and what we are experiencing. To do this with persistence, precision, and intention, takes practice and concentration.

Written All Over
(Exercise Area—Face It—page 169)

Our heads are full of "it." The "it" it is full of, is tension, unease, and unconscious stress. The phrase, "It's written all over your face" refers to our inability to hide what we are feeling or thinking, though we often try to do so. The very act of trying to "put on a face" can be exhausting. All of the senses originate from our head and mind. They are in constant use, including the muscles of the face and the working of our minds.

Pointing The Finger
(Exercise Area—What A Thought—page 153)

Sometimes, we point our finger at someone and angrily say (out loud or to ourselves), "It's your fault. You're the one who started this. You are guilty." At other times, we may point the finger at ourselves; laying on blame, guilt and remorse. "I am so stupid. What was I thinking? I should be punished. I deserve it." Anger and guilt are very persuasive, even more so when we are not acknowledging their presence.

The Heart of the Matter
(Exercise Area—Be Kind—page 140)

The heart is not only the center of the chest, but is also believed to be the center of our emotional life. The heart is where our emotional strings are pulled. It can be overflowing with joy, or breaking from pain and sadness. The heart also picks up chemicals of stress and distress from the rest of the body, including the nervous system and our environment. The emotions, senses and mind are intricately connected. Develop compassion for all.

THIS WEEK

Mindful exercises to reduce stress, increase the ability to self-reflect, and learn how to live with internal and external realities. Bringing one's attention, or awareness, to the present moment with intention.

Doing Something
(Exercise Area—Whatever—page 165)

We sit for a good portion of time every day of our lives. When we are sitting we are usually doing something – watching TV, reading, talking, listening, working, eating, seeing a movie, or sport event. When we take all those activities away and just sit, what happens? Do our bodies, emotions and minds stop working? What is taking place when we pay attention? It may be that there is a lot going on without realizing it.

Beyond Imagination
(Exercise Area—S.E.E.D.I.T.—page 181)

Our consciousness, and what we are conscious of, seems vast and beyond imagination. It is difficult to quantify or pin down. There is so much going on. When we find ways to slow down, pause, and take a breath, there is an opportunity to see that the seemingly endless stream of consciousness is neither endless, nor as vast as we may imagine. Everything is made up of smaller things and so are our mind and thoughts. Being able to differentiate between the major experiences we are aware of; can provide a handle on what is taking place, as it appears, changes, and fades away.

Everything We Need To Know
(Exercise Area—Body Check—page 122)

The body tells us everything we need to know. By paying attention to the changes taking place in our body, and focusing the mind on one aspect, or part, at a time, we begin to notice where we are holding tension, where there is tightness, and/or pain and discomfort. By moving awareness from the bottom of our feet, to the top of our head, we witness the sensations in different parts of the body as they change, intensify, or decrease. As we give attention to the legs, or stomach, we may be pulled away by a thought, or a sensation in another part of the body. Whenever that takes place, come back to the area of focus.

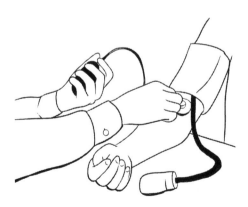

THIS WEEK

Mindful exercises to reduce stress, increase the ability to self-reflect, and learn how to live with internal and external realities. Bringing one's attention, or awareness, to the present moment with intention.

Quiet and Loud
(Exercise Area—Sound Sense—page 133)

Loud and persistent sounds are easily identified. Other sounds are often quieter, less conscious, and go unnoticed. We are most familiar with sounds in our environment and people talking, but there are many internal sound waves as well. Tuning into sound is like making instant oatmeal or hot chocolate – it gives immediate access to one of the senses, which brings us into the present.

Multiple Possibilities
(Exercise Area—The Reporter—page 126)

Sensations and thoughts come and go, like sound. We often ignore them until they are too persistent or intense. The body, including our mind, does not stop because we are unaware of it. When we observe the moment, and use time to identify and observe a thought or a sensation, it brings our awareness into the present and opens multiple possibilities. We recognize whatever is there, and see the filters we lay upon reality.

Powerful Catalysts
(Exercise Area—Emotional Sense—page 151)

Emotions are powerful catalysts that often throw us off kilter, and drive us to act without being aware of where they came from or what we are doing. Emotions, in and of themselves, are neither good or bad, but when we identify with them and believe they will never change, they can take over and blind us to making life-affirming conscious choices. Giving our emotions attention and space can change everything.

Step Outside The Train
(Exercise Area—Boxcars—page 177)

Freight trains have many boxcars, which they pull along the tracks from one location to another. Each boxcar has different content or cargo. Even if two boxcars have similar items, they will not be exactly the same. If you are in one of the boxcars, and there are no windows, you would only be aware of what you see before you. Thoughts are like boxcars. Step outside the train and watch the cars of thought move down the tracks.

THIS WEEK

Mindful exercises to reduce stress, increase the ability to self-reflect, and learn how to live with internal and external realities. Bringing one's attention, or awareness, to the present moment with intention.

What Meets the Eye
(Exercise Area—Come To Your Senses—page 149)

Most people believe that when we close our eyes, that there is nothing to see. Contrary to that assumption, there is a lot to see when our eyelids are closed. The shadows, patterns and colors that filter through our eyelids, or exist between them and the pupil, are constantly moving and changing. The same is true with the other senses. There is much more than meets the eye.

The senses are like a microscope into our being. They can tell us where we are in the moment and what we are, or are not, aware of. Using time as a gift to wake up and see, hear, feel, taste or speak about our experience, in the moment, can literally bring us to our senses.

Rooted To The Present
(Exercise Area—Points of Contact—page 124)

Our bodies are always making contact with something. It can be a material object, a person, or the air. We are not usually aware of the contact being made; let alone the exact point and sensation of that contact. The skin, and nerves that send the signals to our mind, let us know when and how contact is occurring. If we give these points of contact our attention, it can be a grounding act, which roots us to the present.

Fire Of Separation
(Exercise Area—What A Thought—page 153)

What we tell ourselves about life, and our experience of living, is vital information, which can be used to break old patterns and habits. Being aware of our self-talk provides the opportunity to change our responses, and not keep repeating them again and again. Every time we make a judgment about ourselves, or another, we fuel the fire of separation and reinforce that habit, or trait. Perhaps it is time to take another path.

THIS WEEK

Mindful exercises to reduce stress, increase the ability to self-reflect, and learn how to live with internal and external realities. Bringing one's attention, or awareness, to the present moment with intention.

There Is Room
(Exercise Area—Mind In The Clouds—page 159)

Our consciousness is like the sky. Clouds, storms, rain, planes, birds, and countless other objects make their way through space, without the sky believing these material and living things are the sky itself. There is room for everything to come and go. Awareness is like the sky. Our senses, thoughts and experiences are like the weather that comes and goes, neither permanent nor who we are.

Gentle Attention
(Exercise Area—Jelly Belly—page 206)

A soft, relaxed belly tends to spread to the rest of the body and mind, and creates the same sense of relaxation and ease. By focusing on our breath as it enters the body, and the belly expands, and contracts, and feeling it when the air leaves, we give it gentle attention. It isn't something to be forced, and there is no need to breathe rapidly or slowly. Simply observe the belly as it rises and falls.

Far At Sea
(Exercise Area—Ocean Waves—page 161)

Waves begin far out at sea, build, make their way to the shore, and break upon the beach. Trying to stop waves, or redirect them, is not possible. Trying to hold onto, or grasp a wave, is also impossible. Like waves, our sensations, emotions and thoughts form, move, break upon our being and dissipate. We cannot hold onto them or push them away. They are natural phenomena that are part of being human.

Above It All
(Exercise Area—Birds Of A Feather—page 204)

Ah, to be a bird and fly high above it all, watching people, nature and material objects, as they move, sit still and/or interact. Like observing a movie that we are part of, yet not in. Like looking down at earth from an airplane. When we develop mindfulness, and bring awareness to our lives, it can seem as if we are a bird, watching our experiences and reactions to life, without believing that is who we are.

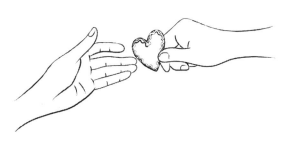

THIS WEEK

Mindful exercises to reduce stress, increase the ability to self-reflect, and learn how to live with internal and external realities. Bringing one's attention, or awareness, to the present moment with intention.

Always Present
(Exercise Area—Breath Of Life—page 131)

The air that we breathe, and the breaths that we take, don't shout for attention, tell us what to do, or judge our lives or behavior. The air that circulates through our bodies is always present and doing its work to keep us alive, even though we are not usually conscious of it doing so. When we give attention to air, and how it interacts with the body on each breath, it helps us to "be" as present and non-judging as it is.

Being Touched
(Exercise Area—Points Of Contact—page 124)

When standing, there are a number of touch points. When lying down, there are more. While sitting, there are at least five specific points of contact where the body is being touched, or touching something. Being aware of these areas, or any one at a given time, and giving them our attention, is a skillful way of coming into the present, reducing stress and relaxing the mind.

The Mind's Programming
(Exercise Area—P.U.F.F.—page 143)

Thinking and having thoughts, is what the mind is programmed to do. We have some influence on the programming, and much of it we do not. In order to not live on automatic, and run the same algorithm over and over, it is helpful to be able to access the mind, and begin to notice when we are thinking, and whether it is about the past, present, future, or fantasy. Bring conscious attention to identifying these differences.

Understanding Conditioning
(Exercise Area—Be Kind—page 140)

Compassion, or kindness, often arises naturally. It can also be an unfamiliar concept, or idea, that we are not able to feel or connect with. Pretending to be kind, while having other thoughts or intentions, doesn't work very well. Learning to be kind and compassionate seems to manifest most clearly when we begin with ourselves and then let it spread to others. It starts with understanding conditioning and our similarities.

THIS WEEK

Mindful exercises to reduce stress, increase the ability to self-reflect, and learn how to live with internal and external realities. Bringing one's attention, or awareness, to the present moment with intention.

It's All Relevant
(Exercise Area—Whatever—page 165)

Bringing awareness to the breath, one of our senses, or the body, provides the opportunity to wake up to what is happening in our heads. We can think about something for hours without realizing that we were distracted, let alone what we were thinking about, or why? Being able to notice the difference between sensations, emotions, or thoughts, is liberating and is the start of having real choice. Whatever is present is relevant.

Endless Loops
(Exercise Area—There Is—page 120)

Thoughts can appear to be endless loops that play in our head again and again. We may try to think of, or do, other things to change the thoughts, or "get rid" of them, and discover that to do so is futile. Thinking is what the mind is supposed to do. Looking closely at our thoughts can help us begin to differentiate and create space between the thoughts and awareness of what they are.

Planning, Understanding or Daydreaming
(Exercise Area—P.U.F.F.—page 143)

"Be prepared! Get it together!" These can be important messages for planning ahead and doing what is possible, but they can also keep us caught tripping about the future, which can heighten anxiety, and keep us ever vigilant for a surprise. We can plan, and prepare for the future, but not control it, though we may think that is what we're doing. Thinking ahead doesn't prepare us for experiencing the present.

"Fantasy" is defined as, "The faculty or activity of imagining things, especially things that are impossible or improbable." Fantasies can be pleasant or unpleasant. Our minds seem to fantasize as a way to escape, create, or provide hope. There are times when we tend to be in fantasyland all the time, and others when we are unaware that we are fantasizing. Are you thinking about the past, present, future, or fantasizing?

THIS WEEK

Mindful exercises to reduce stress, increase the ability to self-reflect, and learn how to live with internal and external realities. Bringing one's attention, or awareness, to the present moment with intention.

At This Moment
(Exercise Area—There Is—page 120)

Let's get real. What's going on right now, right here, at this moment? Not in the world outside, or the environment we are sitting in, but the world and environment within us. What are our bodies experiencing? Is there tightness, discomfort, or unease? Are our legs bouncing up and down? Is our breathing shallow? Bring awareness to the body, senses and mind.

Seeing The Difference
(Exercise Area—S.E.T.—page 155)

When able to see the difference, or differentiate, between the senses, emotions and thoughts, we are able to have some perspective and clarity into our behavior, ideas, feelings and responses. When not paying attention to, and identifying, our physical and mental body, it may seem as if they are all rolled up into a gigantic tidal wave that overwhelms all awareness. Begin to decipher what is being experienced right now.

While Living
(Exercise Area—Good Grief—page 188)

Find someone who does not experience loss or suffering, and they are probably already dead. While living, we all have pain and grief. Every material object, or person, changes and dies. Some things change, or leave us quickly, and others are more drawn out. By identifying, and honoring our losses, we can live more fully in the present and appreciate the moments we have.

Twenty-Four Seven
(Exercise Area—Come To Your Senses—page 149)

The mind is connected to the rest of the body, and vice-a-versa. Sometimes we are so tense, and caught up in our thoughts, that it feels like our minds hurt. Any of the senses, or areas of the body, can become tense with stress, and feel tight, or upset. The chest can feel emotional pain. The ears can hear words of anger or abuse. The body's senses are working 24 x 7. Let them be in a relaxed, loving and compassionate environment.

THIS WEEK

Mindful exercises to reduce stress, increase the ability to self-reflect, and learn how to live with internal and external realities. Bringing one's attention, or awareness, to the present moment with intention.

One Breath At A Time
(Exercise Area—The Old One Two—page 190)

Here it is. Here comes another one; and another, and another. Without breathing we are unconscious of anything. And, most of the time, we are not conscious while we are breathing either. Ironically, one of the quickest ways to become aware of our selves is to pay attention to our breathing, one breath at a time. By doing so, we come intimately into the body and find our rhythm.

On The Surface
(Exercise Area—Face It—page 169)

We hold a lot of tension in our faces. Some of the tension is on the surface and easy to see, and the rest is invisible, as we grit our teeth, and/or tighten the muscles to prevent the world from seeing how we are really feeling, or what we are thinking. Putting on a good face tends to be counterproductive to good health. Simply being aware of the face, and anywhere there is tension, gives us a fresh start, and allows us to "let our hair down."

Put Down The Whip
(Exercise Area—What A Thought—page 153)

Our most severe and constant critic is our self. We tend to believe whatever we tell ourselves, whether it is true, factual, damaging, embellished, or minimized. Someone says something unkind, or we cause someone else to suffer, and we add insult to injury by magnifying the pain given or received, by whipping ourselves for our actions or reactions. We cannot put down the whip until we are aware that it is in our hand.

I Am...
(Exercise Area—Inquiring Mind—page 138)

"Hi. My name is _____. I am a volunteer. I am a teacher. I am a father." Those are labels and roles I may have, but is that who I am? Does what my family, community, society, friends, or colleagues say about me, define me? There are countless activities we are involved in. There are many professions and lifestyles, but who am I beyond my labels and actions? Who am I besides temporary emotions, sensations and thoughts?

THIS WEEK

Mindful exercises to reduce stress, increase the ability to self-reflect, and learn how to live with internal and external realities. Bringing one's attention, or awareness, to the present moment with intention.

It's All We've Got
(Exercise Area—Inside Out—page 175)

Some say the body is a temple. Others say it is simply a biological entity that is the same as the rest of nature. A few people believe it is a vehicle to use from one life to another. Whatever your beliefs, or thoughts are about the body, the reality is that it is all we've got while we're alive. How we treat it, and the mind which keeps it going, is the difference between just surviving and living. Take a close look at the body.

What Makes Us Tick
(Exercise Area—The Urge—page 187)

What is it that makes us tick? What makes us get up every morning and participate in life? Are we looking for something, or someone? Is there a better life with the next job, the new apartment, another city, or a new car? Have I found the friends I'm looking for? Is my spouse (lover) everything I hoped for? Are they what I wanted? Does having a family make me happy and fulfilled? What is this urge, this unquenchable desire?

Taking It For Granted
(Exercise Area—The Casket—page 202)

When the breath stops, we stop. When our bodies are out of breath, they begin to shut down and die. We are breathing as long as we are alive, yet we seldom give any attention to our breath, or observe its progress from outside our body to the inside, and out again. It is a miraculous journey, and process; how we use air to fill our lungs, and provide oxygen to our cells. We take breathing and living for granted.

What Makes Us Human
(Exercise Area—Points of Contact—page 124)

If we've been in our heads, thinking about the past, the future, what we are going to do, what life is all about, or why we are here, it can be reassuring to know there is always a way to come back to the present, to now, and to have contact with our body and what makes us human. Becoming aware of the senses, and sensations on our skin, wherever they are making contact, quickly return us to our home.

THIS WEEK

Mindful exercises to reduce stress, increase the ability to self-reflect, and learn how to live with internal and external realities. Bringing one's attention, or awareness, to the present moment with intention.

The Choices We Make
(Exercise Area—There Is—page 120)

As long as we are alive, there is hope. Hope reminds us that there is always an opportunity for choice. Hope can also be interpreted as intention or possibility. We don't always have control over what happens to us, but we do have a choice in how we respond (or don't respond) to events and situations. The choices we make, in present tense, are partially responsible for what follows. Expanded awareness increases the ability to recognize hope, intention and possibility, by opening our eyes to what is.

Nobody Can Tell Us
(Exercise Area—The Reporter—page 126)

Whatever we are aware of is our reality at the moment. We may not notice everything, but what we see, hear, taste, touch and say, is our undisputed experience. Nobody else can tell us what we are going through, and we can't tell ourselves what we are going through, unless we give it our attention. When not sure what is taking place, call in the reporter, and ask the self what, who, when, where, how and why?

Identify Your Self
(Exercise Area—S.E.T.—page 155)

It is not always easy to tell what is taking place at any given moment. We may be overwhelmed with emotion, off on a train of thought, or preoccupied with a body ache or pain. When we are caught in an experience, and believe that is all that exists or is taking place, we need not despair or give up. Remembering to use the shortcut of S.E.T. provides an immediate tool to pause, differentiate, and identify.

The Courage To Be Mindful
(Exercise Area—B.R.A.V.E.—page 198)

It takes a brave individual to undertake mindful meditation and learn how to be with, identify, and accept whatever is occurring internally and externally. To do so requires concentration, awareness, and the willingness to feel, see, and think about some uncomfortable and distressing aspects of our selves (and others). It also takes commitment and diligence to sit and exercise the mind daily. Be B.R.A.V.E.

A
B.R.A.V.E.
Year

Exercise Area

Exercise Suggestions

- One may sit, stand, walk, or be lying down, to practice these exercises. They can also be done with the eyes closed or open.

- It has been found helpful to close the eyes, with sitting practice, as it takes away one of the senses, so that one's attention can be brought to the rest of the body and mind.

- When sitting, it tends to be most advantages to not sit up too straight (and cause tension), nor slouch too much (and fall asleep). Drop the chin slightly and relax the shoulders.

- There is no specific position in which the hands and feet must be, but it has the most benefit if they can both be completely relaxed while practicing.

- One may discover that they choose to do these exercises before eating a meal, as the corresponding digestive reactions to food are most notable.

- Read each exercise a few times, before practicing, and have a copy on hand to refer to (while learning or teaching).

- The length of time for each mind workout is not as important as doing it daily. Start doing an exercise for 5-10 minutes, to start, and build that time on subsequent days. Like lifting weights, go gradually, at your own pace, and only increase the amount when ready to do so.

- Practice at least one, or two, of these exercises every day at least once, if not several times a day. Remember, they can also be used during any activity or situation.

- Create a private cue, or reminder, to stay fit. It can be anything – a calendar note, an alarm, a phone message, a note on the refrigerator or computer, a band around the wrist.

- Sometimes exercise is tiring, boring, agitated, pleasurable, exhausting, relaxing, or peaceful. Make whatever the experience is, and what you may tell yourself about it, as part of the meditation exercise. Bring awareness and attention to the practice.

There Is

- Close the eyes, and rest the hands and feet.

- Bring awareness to the breath, as it enters and leaves the body.

- Focus attention on sensations in the body, including all the senses.

- At the moment you are aware of a sensation or sense, say, without speaking out loud, "There is sound." "There is pain in the knee." "There is tightness in the chest."

- Note the immediate experience, and awareness of such, by saying, "There is…"

- When aware of thinking, notice thinking. "There is thinking."

- When aware of an emotion, or emotions, make a note. "There is an emotion."

- No need to hold on to a sensation, emotion, or thought; just observe it and say what it is.

- We tend to get lost in sensations, emotions and thoughts without realizing it. By pausing, and every moment or two, saying, "There is…" we provide the opportunity to be aware, and engage in, the present experience.

- "There is…"

- Return to the body and the senses.

- Bring awareness to the breath, as it enters and leaves the body.

- Slowly open the eyes.

Body Check

- Sit comfortably, let the hands relax, and gently close the eyes.

- Become aware of the air surrounding the body; holding the body; giving it life.

- Notice the air as it enters and leaves the body.

- Slowly shift attention to the feet; the bottom of the feet - the sides, top, toes and ankles.

- Bring awareness to the lower legs, knees, thighs and hips - the front, back, and sides of the legs, knees and hips.

- If there is any tightness, or tension, let it be. Let it relax.

- Move attention to the fingers, hands and wrists - the front, back and sides of the fingers, hands and wrists.

- Now, focus on the arms, elbows and shoulders – the front, sides and back of the arms, elbows and shoulders.

- If any discomfort or tightness is noticed, let it be.

- Shift awareness to the back, neck and back of the head – the tailbone, lower, middle and upper back – the neck and back of the skull.

- Wherever pain or tightness resides, let it relax.

- Attend now to the front of the body – the pelvis, belly, chest and throat.

- If there is tension or discomfort, let it be. Notice any shifts, softening, or relaxation.

- Now, bring awareness to the face and the head – the jaw, mouth, nose, eyes, temples, ears, forehead, and top of the skull.

- Bring attention, awareness, to the entire body – the feet, ankles, legs, and hips – the hands, arms, elbows, and shoulders – the tailbone, back, neck and back of skull – the pelvis, belly, chest, throat, face and top of skull.

- Anywhere there is tightness, discomfort or tension, let it be and relax.

- Become aware of the air entering and leaving the body and the surrounding air.

- Slowly open the eyes.

Points of Contact

- Gently close the eyes, sit comfortably and relax the hands.

- Notice the air surrounding the body, and touching the skin – the face, neck, head, hands, and arms.

- Be aware of the breath, as air enters and leaves the body.

- Bring attention to the bottom of the feet, where they are being touched; making contact with the socks, shoes, or the ground. Feel the weight of the feet.

- If there is any tightness, or tension, in the feet, let them relax.

- Now, bring awareness to the bottom, the sit bones – at the point where the butt is making contact with fabric. Notice the weight and pressure.

- If there is any tightness, or tension, in the bottom, let it be.

- Move attention to the hands. What are they touching? Feel the point where they are making contact with another part of the body, clothing, or object.

- If there is any tension or tightness in the hands, let them relax.

- Next, bring awareness to the lips and the place where the bottom lip is touching the top lip.

- If there is any tightness or tension in the lips, or around the mouth, let it be.

- Shift attention to the eyes, at the exact spot where the upper lid touches the bottom lid.

- If there is any tension or tightness with, or around the eyes, relax.

- Be aware of the points of contact for the bottom of the feet, the butt, the hands, the lips and the eyelids. If there is any tension or tightness let it be. Relax.

- Return to the breath, as air enters and leaves the body.

- Feel the air surrounding the body and touching the skin – the face, neck, head, hands, and arms.

- Gently open the eyes.

The Reporter

- Begin by gently closing the eyes, sitting comfortably, and letting the hands relax.

- Feel the air surrounding the body and entering with each breath. Breathe naturally. No need to breathe quickly or slowly.

- Bring attention to the body, as it begins to relax and settle.

- Notice any tension in the body and let it be.

- Recall a recent, or past, situation that first comes to mind. Use a good reporter's tool, and ask yourself what, who, where, how, when, and why.

- How were other people, or one individual, behaving? How were you behaving or reacting?

- Investigate, and look closely, at the behaviors you discovered. There is no need to judge, blame or compare.

- Slowly, bring attention back to the body, noticing any tense areas and letting it relax.

- Focus awareness on the breath, as it enters and leaves the body. Feel the air around the body and slowly open the eyes.

- Be a reporter with any past, present, or future experience. Look closely. Take notes. Pay attention.

S.T.O.P.

(S = Stop, T = Take a breath, O = Observe,
P = Proceed with awareness)

- Close the eyes gently, and let the legs and hands relax.

- Become aware of the air surrounding and touching the body.

- Follow the breath, as it enters and leaves the body.

- By sitting, and closing the eyes, you have stopped. By becoming aware of the air surrounding and entering the body, you have taken a breath.

- Now, be aware of the senses and body sensations. Do you hear something… feel something… taste something? Is there tightness or tension somewhere in the body?

- Shift awareness to thoughts and thinking. Is there a thought, or a number of thoughts, that just crossed the mind? Was there an idea about the future, or a memory of the past? Has one of the senses triggered some thoughts, or a thought triggered a reaction in the body?

- By giving attention to the body, its senses, and then to any thoughts that arise, you have observed and proceeded with awareness.

- Pause, tune in, see what is taking place, and then repeat it. Stop, take a breath, observe, and proceed with awareness.

- Follow the breath, as it enters and leaves the body.

○   Become aware of the air surrounding and touching the body.

○   Gently open the eyes and continue to S.T.O.P. throughout the day.

R.A.R.E.

(R=Recognize, A=Allow, R=Review, E=Envision)

- Gently close the eyes, and let the hands and legs relax.

- Notice the air surrounding and touching the body.

- Feel the air, as it enters and leaves the body, one breath at a time.

- If any thoughts or emotions arise, give them complete attention. What is the content? Is one thought or emotion leading to another? As soon as you are aware of being "lost in thought", or a strong emotion, return to being an observer.

- By bringing awareness to the breath, and observing emotions and thoughts, as they are, we are recognizing and allowing them to be, without trying to control, or manipulate the experience.

- Observing, and looking into, sensations, emotions, or thoughts, is the essence of how to mindfully review and see any connections.

- Shift awareness to thoughts and thinking. Is there a thought, or a number of thoughts, that just crossed the mind? Was there an idea about the future, or a memory of the past? Has one of the senses triggered some thoughts, or a thought triggered a reaction in the body?

- Returning to the breath, recognizing what is taking place, allowing the content, or experience, to be;

and closely observing and investigating what arises (and passes away), creates the conditions for less attachment and connection to what is taking place, and the freedom to envision ourselves with awareness.

- Feel the air as it enters and leaves the body, one breath at a time.

- Notice the air surrounding and touching the body.

- Gently open the eyes and continue to utilize R.A.R.E. as a daily practice.

Breath of Life

- Close the eyes, and let the body settle.

- Feel the air surrounding and touching the body; notice where it makes contact with the skin. It may feel hot, cool, or prickly.

- Follow the air, as it enters the body, through the nose and/ or mouth, down the throat, and into the lungs, with each inhale, and as it returns from the lungs, up the throat and out the nose and/or mouth, upon each exhale.

- Each breath is a life preserver for the body. Each breath brings in fresh air, circulates and absorbs it, and then sends it back into the atmosphere to be used again.

- Breathe naturally. Let the body go at its own pace. There is no need to breathe quickly, or try to force it to slow down.

- Breath is life. Without it, the body and the consciousness it contains, cannot live or interact with the senses and surroundings. We seldom give the breath any attention. As long as we are alive, it works on automatic, but has great effect on our stress and health.

- Keep coming back to the breath. Focus attention on its complete path, from inhalation to exhalation, or on any one point along the way. If the strongest connection is at the tip of the nose, then maintain awareness of it entering and leaving at that point. If the back of the throat, or the expanding and contracting of the lungs, are stronger points of contact, then be aware of one of those areas with each breath.

- Follow the air, one breath at a time, as it enters and leaves the body. If thoughts, emotions, or other sensations come into awareness, return to the breath as soon as they are noticed - one breath at a time.

- Feel the air surrounding and touching the body; notice where it makes contact with the skin.

- Breathe and open the eyes slowly.

Sound Sense

- Close the eyes and relax the arms, hands and legs.

- Become aware of the air surrounding and holding the body.

- Follow the air, as it enters and leaves the body, one breath at a time.

- Bring attention to the sound sense – to hearing, listening.

- Listen to any noise, or sounds, from the environment.

- Listen to any noise, or sounds, that are within.

- Be aware of both external and internal sound.

- Notice the sound, when you are first aware of it, and when it leaves awareness.

- Keep giving attention to sound. If other senses or thoughts come into awareness, make a note of what it is, and return to sound.

- Can the sound sense differentiate between soft, medium and loud? Notice changes in the sound being heard. Are there multiple sounds coming into awareness at once, or is it one at a time?

- Whatever else comes into awareness, come back to sound. Concentrate on sound.

- Follow the air, as it enters and leaves the body, one breath at a time.

- Become aware of the air surrounding and holding the body.

- Slowly open the eyes and continue bringing awareness to the sound sense.

S.E.E.I.T.

(S = Senses, E = Emotions, E = Emptiness,
I = Intentions, T = Thoughts)

- Gently close the eyes, and relax the rest of the body.

- Feel the air surrounding the body, and the points at which it is contacting the skin.

- Become aware of breathing in and out, as the air enters and leaves the body. Let the body breathe naturally: no need to speed up or slow down.

- There is nowhere else to be and nothing to do. Be right here, right now.

- Every moment we are alive, we can use S.E.E.I.T.

- S.E.E.I.T. encompasses almost any experience that is possible, and helps us differentiate and recognize what is taking place.

- Keep following the breath and become aware of the senses, the S. in S.E.E.I.T. Notice sensations in the body, sounds, taste, and sight (when the eyes are open). Keep awareness on the senses, as they come and go.

- If sidetracked on another experience, return to the breath and the senses, or any one of the senses.

- Be aware of breathing in and breathing out.

- Now, include any emotions that come to attention. Be aware of the senses, and the E. in S.E.E.I.T. – emotions.

These may include sadness, joy, anger, fear, love, guilt, or anxiety.

- Like senses, there is no need to get rid of, or hold on to, any emotion. Be aware of what is there, and acknowledge it as it arises and passes away.

- Breathe in and breathe out.

- If in a void, or a sense of emptiness is present, then identify it as such. The second E. in S.E.E.I.T. With emptiness, there is no awareness of any specific emotion, sensation, thought or intention.

- Come back to the breath.

- Bring attention to the present experience and include any intentions that come into awareness. The I. in S.E.E.I.T. Intentions are similar to desires. An intention is something one wants, or wishes to happen.

- Breathing in and breathing out, give full attention to the senses, emotions, emptiness, and intentions - note which you are aware of at this moment. Watch them come and go.

- Now, include thinking, or thoughts. The T. in S.E.E.I.T. Was that a thought, or an emotion? What was I just thinking? What sensation am I aware of? Was that another thought?

- Use S.E.E.I.T. to clarify and recognize, what is coming into awareness, at any given moment.

- If everything feels intense, or overwhelming, break it down with S.E.E.I.T. Is this a sense, an emotion, a feeling of emptiness, an intention, or a thought?

🗩 Come back to the breath. Breathe in and breathe out.

🗩 Be aware of the air around the body, and the points where it is felt.

🗩 Slowly open the eyes and continue using S.E.E.I.T. throughout the day.

Inquiring Mind

- With the eyes gently closed, become aware of the breath.

- Notice the air, as the breath enters and leaves the body, one at a time.

- There is always air surrounding and passing through the body. Give it attention.

- Feel the air as it touches the tip of the nose, goes down the throat and into the lungs, then feel it as it reverses and leaves the body upon exhale.

- By giving the breath attention, we give the body attention. By giving the body attention, we are able to then see emotions and thoughts, which come and go within our physical body and mind.

- Make a note of any sensations, emotions, or thoughts, which are coming into awareness.

- Return to the breath, with each inhale and exhale.

- Bring attention to any emotions, or thoughts, which come into consciousness. What do they consist of? Where do they come from? Are they connected to any previous event, emotion or thought?

- Sensations, emotions and thoughts are always within context. They are interlaced with conditioning, past experiences, habits, and self-preservation.

- Beyond the labels, cultural definitions and current circumstances, who are we? Who, or what is it that is aware, or mindful, of these sensations, emotions and thoughts?

- More importantly, what are we telling ourselves about what we think and feel? The messages we give to ourselves can be just as important and impactful as what we are experiencing and aware of.

- Look deeply. Keep asking the question, "Who am I?" and "What am I telling myself?"

- Now, come back to the breath, and feel it entering and leaving the body.

- Notice the air surrounding the body and all the points at which it makes contact.

- Open the eyes slowly. Keep the inquiring mind active.

Be Kind

- Close the eyes softly and let the hands, arms and legs relax.

- Feel the air that surrounds, and holds the body, giving it life and space.

- Notice where the body is touched by the air.

- Breathe in this nurturing substance, feel it circulate through the lungs, and back into the space that surrounds you. No need to force the air. Let it breathe for you, as the body requires.

- Bring awareness to the senses. Is there a sound, smell, taste, or sensation that is noticeable? If so, embrace it as such. "There is a sound." "There is a smell." "There is a sensation."

- Now, bring awareness to the emotions. Is there a feeling of sadness, anger, joy, helplessness, or contentment? If so, embrace it. "There is sadness." "There is anger." "There is happiness." "There is loneliness."

- Shift attention to thoughts. Is there a thought about the past, present, or future? What is it? What are you thinking? If a thought comes into awareness, embrace it as, "There is a thought about the past." "There is a thought about the future." "There is a thought about the present."

Our senses, emotions and thoughts are part of the human experience, though they do not define who we are. Most of what we experience is out of our control.   It is our unawareness, and inattention, that create additional pain or suffering, sometimes, as much as the direct experience of life itself.

What we tell ourselves matters. What are you aware of right now? If it is a sensation, emotion, or thought, embrace it. Now, see if you can decipher what you may be telling yourself about that sensation, emotion, or thought.

Be gentle with what you say, whether it is out loud to someone else, or to yourself. Words are energy and energy affects everything. Be kind with the messages you give the self. Blame, guilt, and anger, at oneself or another, are not always necessary or of use.

Be compassionate with the past, present and future.

Be forgiving with sensations, emotions, or thoughts, which have arisen from past inattention, ignorance, or judgment.

The heart is both strong and fragile. Our bodies are strong and fragile. Our emotions and thoughts are strong and fragile. See them honestly for what they are.

Be Kind

Embrace kindness and compassion into your heart and let it spread.

Come back to the senses, to the body.

Breathe in the nurturing air, feel it circulate through the lungs, and back into the space that surrounds you.

- Feel the air touching, holding and embracing the body, giving it life and space.

- Slowly open the eyes and continue being kind to one and all.

P.U.F.F.

(P = Past, U = Unfolding, F = Fantasy, F = Future)

- Gently close the eyes, and let the hands and legs relax.

- Notice the air surrounding and touching the body.

- Feel the air, as it enters and leaves the body, one breath at a time.

- When thoughts arise, give them complete attention. Be an observer of thought. What is the content? Is it a thought about the past, present, a fantasy, or the future?

- Thoughts about the past can include memories, events, people, or trying to figure out what happened, or took place. Thoughts that are in the present, and unfolding, might include interpretations of the environment, other individuals, or making connections. Thoughts that are fantasy involve unrealistic, hypothetical, or creative thinking. Thoughts pertaining to the future involve planning, preparing, and organizing.

- Observing, and looking into thoughts, is the essence of how to mindfully investigate and see how thoughts from the past, present, fantasy and future, influence and shape one another.

- Returning to the breath, recognizing what thought is and when it is taking place, gives some space between being caught in our thoughts, and being able to observe its contents.

- Feel the air as it enters and leaves the body, one breath at a time.

- Follow the breath, as it enters and leaves the body.

- Notice the air surrounding and touching the body.

- Gently open the eyes and continue to use P.U.F.F. as part of your daily routine.

Weather Report

- Gently close the eyes and make yourself comfortable.

- Notice the air surrounding the body, always changing and always there.

- Bring awareness to this same air, as it enters the body with each breath. Notice the chest as it rises and falls.

- Scan the body from head to toe. Wherever there is tension, tightness or discomfort, relax, and let it be.

- Sense any emotions, or thoughts, as they come and go.

- Now, like a weather report, tell yourself what you are experiencing. "There is a strong emotion of sadness, which I'm feeling in the chest." "There is a thought about Jane, and what she said to me this morning." "There is another thought about Jane." "The chest area is relaxed." "There is a joyful sensation around the heart." "Here comes a sensation in the stomach and a following thought that I'm hungry."

- By observing the body, the emotions, and thoughts, like a weather report, space is created between the content and self-identification with it. This space can provide clarity and understanding about who we are, how we are conditioned, and how we respond.

- Continue to observe and report. What is happening? What is taking place? What is changing? How does one moment affect the next?

- Now, scan the body from head to toe. Wherever there is tension, tightness or discomfort, relax, and let it be.

- Be aware of the air, as it enters the body with each breath. Notice the chest as it rises and falls.

- Slowly open the eyes and continue to monitor the internal weather, and report several times throughout the day.

Like a Mountain

- Sit comfortably, with the bottom touching the chair, cushion, floor, or ground.

- Have the hands in a position in which they can completely relax.

- Gently close the eyes.

- Envision the body as a mountain. The legs and hips are the base, the trunk and arms are the slopes, and the head is the peak.

- Mountains are solid. Mountains are grounded. Mountains rarely move.

- Now, bring awareness to the air surrounding you, a mountain, as it touches the skin. It may be hot, cold, prickly, or neutral.

- Feel what you are wearing, as it touches the skin. Your clothes and hair are like trees and plants on a mountainside.

- Your skin is like the topsoil that covers the mountain.

- Like the sound of birds and animals visiting the mountain, listen to the sounds that surround you, as they arise, enter your awareness, and fade away.

- Bring awareness to other sensations in the body, and

notice any of the senses.

💭 Bring awareness to any emotions that are coming and going. Observe them closely.

💭 Bring awareness to thoughts, as they come and go.

💭 Sensations, emotions, and thoughts are like the earth, plants, trees, animals and weather, which visit the mountain. Some stay for decades, and others for days or minutes.

💭 A mountain stays a mountain. It rarely changes, even though what touches it, and passes by, is constantly changing. A mountain does not deny what comes into its realm; it embraces it and lets it run its course.

💭 Use awareness and concentration to be a mountain to yourself. Strong winds, thoughts, sensations, or emotional avalanches, affect us, but do not define our core, or move our base.

💭 Now, bring awareness to the air surrounding you, a mountain, as it touches the skin.

💭 Your awareness and attention is the core of the mountain. Use them to observe the internal and external environment.

💭 Slowly open the eyes, and gently stretch the body.

Come To Your Senses

- Gently close the eyes, so the other senses have all the attention. Feel the air surrounding the body, and where it touches the skin.

- Notice where the air enters the body, with each breath, at the tip of the nose.

- Follow one breath at a time, as it makes its way down the throat, into the lungs, and then back out the throat and the tip of the nose (or mouth).

- Bring awareness to the feet, and slowly move attention to each part of the body, to the top of the head. Anywhere that tension is noticed, let it be. Any area that feels tight; let it relax. Any part of the body that is uncomfortable, or restless, let it be at ease.

- Continue following the breath as it enters and leaves the body, one at a time.

- Now, shift awareness to sound. Any sound that comes into awareness (externally or internally), make a mental note, and say to the self, "There is a door closing." "There is someone speaking." "There is a high-pitch ring in my ear."

- Continue following the breath, as it enters and leaves the body, one at a time.
- Now, shift awareness to smell. Any smell that comes into awareness (externally or internally), make a mental note,

and say to the self, "There is a body odor." "There is the smell of coffee." "There is a sweet smell."

- Continue following the breath, as it enters and leaves the body, one at a time.

- Now, shift awareness to speech. Anything you think about saying, make a mental note, and say to the self, "There is something I want to say." "There is something wrong." "There is something I don't understand."

- Continue following the breath, as it enters and leaves the body, one at a time.

- Now, shift awareness to taste. Anything with the sense of taste that comes into awareness, make a mental note, and say to the self, "There is a salty taste." "There is a sour taste." "There is a sweet taste."

- Continue following the breath, as it enters and leaves the body, one at a time.

- Bring awareness to the feet, and slowly move attention to each part of the body, to the top of the head. Anywhere that tension is noticed, let it be and relax.

- Follow one breath at a time, as it makes its way down the throat, into the lungs, and then back out the throat, and the tip of the nose (or mouth).

- Feel the air surrounding the body, and notice where it touches the skin.

- Slowly open the eyes and continue to be aware of the senses, moment to moment.
- Relax the hands and feet, and gently close the eyes.

Emotional Sense

Feel each breath, as it enters and leaves the body. Feel the stomach and chest rise, and fall with each inhalation and exhalation.

With each breath, let the body relax, and be at ease.

Be aware of any sensations that come to be – a sore knee, a tight chest, and ache in the back, agitation with a leg moving. Acknowledge whatever comes into awareness. No need to change it, get rid of it, or try to hold onto it.

By shining the light of awareness on a sensation, and giving it close attention, it begins to change of its own accord. Be a witness to its transition, as it increases or decreases in duration, intensity, or context.

With each breath, let the body relax, and be at ease.

Now, be aware of any feelings that come into consciousness – love, fear, tenderness, anger, sadness, helplessness; joy. Acknowledge whatever comes into awareness. No need to change the feeling, get rid of it, hold onto it or judge it.

By shining the light of awareness on an emotion, and giving it close attention, it begins to change, and shift, of its own accord. Be a witness, an observer, to its transition, as it increases, or decreases in duration, intensity, or context.

⚬ What may at first appear to be a bundle of emotions all clumped together is often one after another. Feel, observe, and investigate what emotion preceded the one presently being experienced. For example, what first appears, or feels like anger, is usually preceded by sadness, loss of control, and/or helplessness.

⚬ How we interpret an emotional experience, and the message we give ourselves about what we are feeling, is just as vital to be aware of.

⚬ Emotions are often felt in the body. If there is a reaction in the body, with a corresponding emotion, make a note. Emotions affect the body and vice-a-versa.

⚬ With each breath, let the body relax, and be at ease.

⚬ Feel each breath, as it enters and leaves the body. Feel the stomach and chest rise, and fall, upon inhalation and exhalation.

⚬ Slowly open the eyes. Check in with your emotional sense frequently.

What A Thought

☁   Relax the hands and feet, and gently close the eyes.

☁   Feel each breath, as it enters and leaves the body. Feel the stomach and chest rise, and fall.

☁   With each breath, let the body relax, and be at ease.

☁   Be aware of any sensations that come to be. Acknowledge whatever comes into awareness. No need to change it, get rid of it, or try to hold onto it.

☁   By shining the light of awareness on a sensation, and giving it close attention, it begins to change of its own accord.

☁   With each breath, let the body relax, and be at ease.

☁   Now, be aware of any thoughts that come into consciousness – thoughts about others, about things, about the self. Acknowledge whatever thoughts come to mind - no need to change them, get rid of them, or judge them.

☁   By shining the light of awareness on a thought, and giving it close attention, it is easier to see where it came from, and how it is connected to the senses and past conditioning.

☁   What may at first appear to be a bundle of thoughts all clumped together, is often one after another. Investigate what thought preceded the one you are presently aware of.

153

Thoughts can run on and on. When stepping back and observing thoughts closely it becomes apparent that they are connected.

How we interpret our thoughts, and the messages we tell ourselves about what we are thinking, is just as vital to be aware of, as are thoughts themselves.

Anxious, or fearful, thoughts often have a corresponding reaction in the body. Thoughts are a form of energy and can affect the body and vice-a-versa.

With each breath, let the body relax, and be at ease.

Feel each breath, as it enters and leaves the body. Feel the stomach and chest rise, and fall.

Slowly open the eyes. Be aware of the mind and when, and what you are thinking.

S.E.T.

(S = Senses, E = Emotions, T = Thoughts)

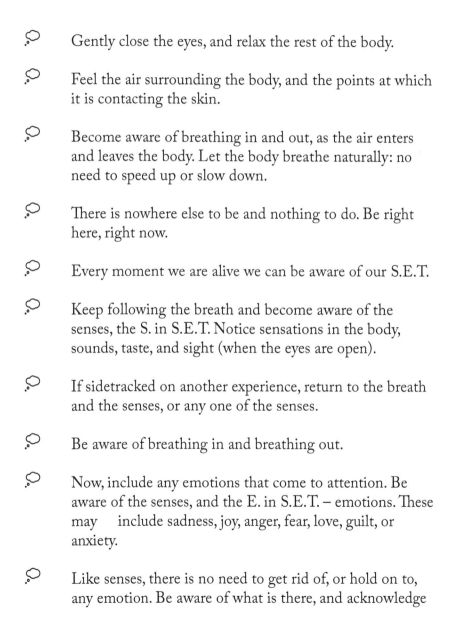

Gently close the eyes, and relax the rest of the body.

Feel the air surrounding the body, and the points at which it is contacting the skin.

Become aware of breathing in and out, as the air enters and leaves the body. Let the body breathe naturally: no need to speed up or slow down.

There is nowhere else to be and nothing to do. Be right here, right now.

Every moment we are alive we can be aware of our S.E.T.

Keep following the breath and become aware of the senses, the S. in S.E.T. Notice sensations in the body, sounds, taste, and sight (when the eyes are open).

If sidetracked on another experience, return to the breath and the senses, or any one of the senses.

Be aware of breathing in and breathing out.

Now, include any emotions that come to attention. Be aware of the senses, and the E. in S.E.T. – emotions. These may include sadness, joy, anger, fear, love, guilt, or anxiety.

Like senses, there is no need to get rid of, or hold on to, any emotion. Be aware of what is there, and acknowledge it as it arises and passes away.

- Breathe in and breathe out. Give complete attention to the senses and emotions that you are aware of at this moment. Watch them come and go.

- Now, include thinking, or thoughts. The T. in S.E.T. Was that a thought, or an emotion? What was I just thinking? What sensation am I aware of? Was that another thought?

- What is coming into awareness, and what is happening in the moment? If everything feels intense, or overwhelming, break it down with S.E.T. Is this a sense, an emotion, or a thought?

- Now, come back to the breath. Breathe in and breathe out.

- Be aware of the air around the body, and the points where it is felt.

- Slowly open the eyes and continue using S.E.T. whenever needed.

Head to Toe

- Sit comfortably, let the hands relax, and gently close the eyes.

- Become aware of the air surrounding the body; holding the body; giving it life.

- Notice the air as it enters and leaves through the nostrils.

- Slowly shift attention to the face and the head – the top of the skull, forehead, ears, temples, eyes, nose, mouth, and jaw.

- Anywhere there is tightness, discomfort or tension, let it be and relax.

- Now, become aware of the front of the body – the throat, chest, belly, and pelvis.

- If there is tension or discomfort, let it be. Notice any softening, or relaxation.

- Shift awareness to the back of the head, neck, and back – the back of the skull, the neck – the upper and middle of the back, the lower back, and tailbone.

- Wherever pain, or tightness resides, let it relax.

- Now focus on the shoulders, elbows, and arms - around every side.

- Move attention to the wrists, hands and fingers - the front, back and sides.

- If any discomfort or tightness is noticed, let it be.

- Bring awareness to the hips, thighs, knees, and lower legs. The front, back, and sides of the hips, knees and legs.

- Notice the ankles, feet, and toes - all sides - top and bottom.

- If there is any tightness, or tension, let it be. Let it relax.

- Bring attention, awareness, to the entire body – the top of the skull, the face, the throat, chest, belly and pelvis – the shoulders, elbows, arms, and hands – the back of the skull, neck, back, and tailbone – the hips, legs, ankles, feet, and toes.

- Anywhere there is tightness, discomfort or tension, let it be and relax.

- Become aware of the air entering and leaving the body into the surrounding air.

- Slowly open the eyes.

Mind in the Clouds

- Let the body relax and the eyes close.

- Sit comfortably.

- Feel the touch of the air surrounding the body on the skin.

- Be aware of the air as it enters the body.

- The air we breathe is the same air that is in the sky.

- The air we breathe is the same air that is blown, like clouds, by the wind.

- The air we breathe moves, changes, and comes and goes, of its own accord.

- Sensations, emotions and thoughts are similar to air and clouds in the sky. They come into being by internal and external factors, conditioning and circumstances, and dissipate, or blow away.

- Let the mind be an open sky and thoughts be clouds.

- When a thought enters awareness, notice when it is there, what shape it takes, and where it goes.

- No need to try to change the thought cloud, or blow it away. It comes and goes at its own pace.

- If you find you have been drifting on some thought clouds

unaware, than the moment you realize it, you are once again the sky of awareness.

There is no other place to be. There is nothing else to do. Just sit and watch the thoughts come and go.

Slowly, bring attention back to the breath - the same air that is in the sky.

Be aware of the air, as it enters the body.

Feel the touch of the air surrounding the body on the skin.

Open the eyes slowly. Whenever life feels confined, or closed in, remember the sky, the consciousness within which the clouds of thought come and go.

Ocean Waves

- Let the body relax and the eyes close.

- Sit comfortably.

- Feel the touch of the air surrounding the body on the skin.

- Be aware of the air as it enters the body.

- The air we breathe is the same air that blows across the oceans.

- The air we breathe, like waves on the ocean, enters the body, circulates, and is then released to be recycled.

- Sensations, emotions and thoughts are similar to ocean waves. They come into being by internal and external factors, conditioning and circumstances, make their way to shore, crash upon the land, and dissipate back into the sea.

- Let the mind be like the open sea, and thoughts like waves.

- When a thought enters awareness, notice when it is there, what shape it takes, and where it goes.

- No need to try to change the thought wave, or push it away. It comes and goes at its own pace.

- If you find you have been drifting on some thoughts in the open sea, unaware, the moment you realize it, you are once again an ocean of awareness.

There is no other place to be. There is nothing else to do. Just sit and watch the thoughts come and go.

Slowly, bring attention back to the breath - the same air that blows across the oceans.

Be aware of the air, as it enters the body.

Feel the touch of the air surrounding the body on the skin.

Open the eyes slowly. If in the grasp of anxiety, or confusion, remember that they are thoughts, which come and go, like waves on the ocean.

Time Trip

- Sit comfortably, gently close the eyes, and focus on the breath.

- Bring attention to the breath as it enters and leaves the body.

- Notice the pause, or space, that follows the out breath (exhalation), previous to the in breath (inhalation).

- It is often within this space between breaths, that the mind rushes in to fill the moment with thought.

- If a thought arises, and you are aware of it, make note of "thinking". "There is thinking".

- Return awareness to the breath, as it enters and leaves the body, and thoughts that come and go.

- Now, try to remember what you were thinking 1 minute ago.

- What were you thinking an hour ago?

- What were you thinking 24 hours ago?

- Return to the breath, and notice any thoughts that arise.

- Now, think about the future. What will you be thinking a minute from now?

- What will you be thinking an hour from now?

- What will be your thoughts 24 hours from now?

- Come back to the breath.

- This moment is the only moment in which we can be aware of our thoughts – right here – right now.

- This moment is the only moment in which we can make change, by being aware of the present, and making informed choices with insight.

- Notice the breath, as it enters and leaves the body.

- Slowly open the eyes and continue to observe when your thoughts are caught time tripping in the past or future.

Whatever

- Sit back, close the eyes, and relax.

- What is happening, taking place? What's going on?

- Whatever it is, give it your attention.

- Notice anything in the environment, or any of the senses being engaged?

- Whatever it is, give it your attention.

- Are there thoughts about the past, present or future?

- Whatever it is, give it your attention.

- Do you feel any emotions about anything?

- Whatever it is, give it your attention.

- Observe whatever comes into awareness – be they pleasant, unpleasant, or neutral.

- Sensations, sounds, tastes, anxiety, love, fear, confusing thoughts, clarity, or frustration.

- Whatever it is, give it your complete attention - right here, right now.

- What is happening, taking place? What's going on?

○ Now sit up, open the eyes, and continue to relax into the moment – whatever that may be.

Can You Count To Ten?

- Gently close the eyes, and let the hands relax.

- Notice the air surrounding the body, and the areas on the skin where it is being touched by the air.

- Follow the air, as it makes its way into and out of the body, one breath at a time.

- Now, begin counting the breaths, starting at one, and ending at ten.

- At the end of each exhalation, right before taking the next breath, begin with one, and proceed at the end of the following breath with two.

- Continue counting in-between breaths, until having counted to ten, and then begin again with one.

- Every time that you become aware of having lost count, or being caught in thought, begin again at one.

- It doesn't matter how many times you start over, or whether you make it to ten without the mind wandering, or losing count.

- The very act of giving attention to the breath, moment to moment, helps develop concentration, which goes hand in hand with awareness.

- Breathe in. Breathe out. One. Breathe in. Breathe out. Two. Breathe in. Breathe out. Three.

- Keep coming back to the breath, as it enters and leaves.

- At the very instant you notice having been lost in thought, or forgetting what number you are on, and coming back to the breath, you have returned to awareness.

- Continue counting in-between breaths, until having counted ten, and then begin again with one.

- Follow the air, as it makes its way into and out of the body, one breath at a time.

- Notice the air surrounding the body, and the areas on the skin where it is being touched by the air.

- Slowly open the eyes. Come back to the breath, whenever you remember to do so.

Face It

- Sit comfortably, and gently close the eyes.

- Let the hands and legs relax.

- Notice the air surrounding the body and the areas on the face the air is touching.

- The air may feel cool, hot, humid, prickly, or just caressing the face lightly.

- With each breath, feel the air at the tip of the nose, as it enters and exits.

- Be aware of the chin, and the jaw. Let them relax.

- Be aware of the spot where the upper jawbone and the lower jawbone come together, on the side of the head. Let it be.

- Be aware of the side of the head, the temples, and ears. Let them relax.

- Now, be aware of the mouth and nose, the area around the mouth and nose, and let it be.

- Bring awareness to the eyes, and the area around the eyes, and let them relax.

- Shift awareness to the forehead, and let it be.

- Bring awareness to the entire face – the chin and jaw – the jaw joint and temples – the mouth and nose – the eyes – the forehead.

- Anywhere there is tension, or tightness, let it be and relax.

- No need to impress, be happy or sad, hold it together, or "put on a face".

- Let everything relax and be as it is.

- With each breath, feel the air at the tip of the nose, as it enters and exits.

- The air may feel cool, hot, humid, prickly, or just caressing the face lightly.

- Notice the air surrounding the body and the areas on the face the air is touching.

- Open the eyes gently.

Hands Down

- Sit comfortably, and gently close the eyes.

- Let the hands and legs relax.

- Notice the air surrounding the body and the areas on the hands the air is touching.

- With each breath, feel the air, as it enters and exits the body.

- Now, bring awareness to the hands.

- Be aware of the top of the hands, and let them be.

- Be aware of the side of the side of the hands, and let them relax.

- Now, be aware of the bottom of the hands, and let them be.

- Shift awareness to the fingers – the top, bottom and sides, and let them relax.

- Notice if there is any tension, tightness, soreness, or nervous energy in the hands.

- There is nothing the hands need to do right now. Nothing they need to grasp, touch, push away, pick up, put down, or move.

- Let the hands be at ease. Let the tops, sides, and bottoms of the hands and fingers completely, and totally, relax.

- Notice the air surrounding the body and the areas on the hands the air is touching.

- With each breath, feel the air, as it enters and exits the body.

- Gently open the eyes.

Fresh Air

- Close the eyes.

- Air surrounds the body, making contact with the skin.

- The air enters the body, at the tip of the nose, and makes its way to the lungs.

- The lungs spread oxygen to the system, and sends the remaining air back past the tip of the nose, (or mouth), and into the surrounding space.

- Each breath of air is a new beginning and ending.

- Each breath of air gives life, and powers the mind and body to live.

- With each new breath that enters the body, is the opportunity to be aware.

- As each breath leaves the body, is the opportunity to relax and be at ease.

- Every breath is recycled, recharged and reused by other living beings.

- We all live in the same atmosphere and breathe the same air.

- The amount of air we can breathe in our atmosphere is

finite.

- Fresh air is invaluable and the life-blood of all living things.

- Each breath is precious. Each moment is precious.

- Let the body breathe to its own rhythm. No need to speed up, or slow down.

- Take a breath and release.

- Take another breath and release - moment to moment.

- The air enters the body, at the tip of the nose, and makes its way to the lungs.

- Air surrounds the body, making contact with the skin.

- Breathe in and breathe out.

- Open the eyes.

Inside Out

- Close the eyes.

- Feel the surrounding air, as it touches the skin.

- Envision, or imagine, the body from the inside out.

- How our body functions, is seldom given any attention, unless something is not working properly, or out of sync.

- Envision air, as it enters the body, at the tip of the nose, down the throat, and into the lungs.

- Feel the lungs rise and fall, as they spread oxygen throughout the respiratory system.

- Follow the breath of air, as it travels back out the throat, and past the tip of the nose, (or mouth), into the surrounding space.

- Now, put a hand on the heart, and feel it beating – pumping blood to all parts of the body.

- The heart keeps a rhythm to replenish and nourish cells throughout the body.

- Imagine the blood coursing through the arteries and veins, as it spreads and revitalizes the circulatory system.

- Now, envision a glass of water or bite of food, as it travels down the throat, into their corresponding areas of the stomach, kidneys and intestines, before making their way through the process of elimination.

One system cannot operate without the other. The respiratory, circulatory, and digestive organisms are inter-dependent.

Now, focus on the skeletal structure, the bones that connect from top to bottom – giving us shape, the ability to sit, stand, and move.

Feel the bones, under the skin – some large, some curved, some small.

Now, imagine the nerve network, as it sends messages within the brain, and from the brain, to the rest of the body. Moving at lightning speed to act, react, think, understand, move, and reason.

Each of these systems (respiratory, circulatory, digestive, skeletal, and nervous) has millions of cells co-operating, and working together.

All the cells affect one another within the body's closed system. When one area is relaxed, balanced, and attentive, it helps the other systems to function with ease.

Now, envision the air, as it enters the body, circulates and leaves.

Feel the surrounding air, as it touches the skin – skin that protects and encapsulates everything within.

Open the eyes, and appreciate the marvelous body within which we have our being.

Boxcars

🗨 Relax the hands and feet, and gently close the eyes.

🗨 Feel each breath, as it enters and leaves the body. Feel the stomach and chest rise, and fall, upon inhalation and exhalation.

🗨 With each breath, let the body relax and be at ease.

🗨 Be aware of any sensations that come to be. Acknowledge whatever comes into awareness.

🗨 By shining the light of awareness on a sensation, and giving it close attention, it begins to change of its own accord.

🗨 With each breath, let the body relax, and be at ease.

🗨 Now, be aware of any thoughts that come into consciousness. Acknowledge whatever thoughts come to mind.

🗨 By shining the light of awareness on thoughts, it is easier to stay focused in the present, and notice when the mind has been caught in a freight car of thinking.

🗨 What may at first appear to be a bundle of thoughts all clumped together, is often one after another. Investigate what thought preceded the one you are presently aware of. Thoughts can run on and on.

- When stepping back and observing thoughts closely, it becomes apparent that they are often connected to some internal or external stimulus.

- Most of the time, we are caught in one drama after another. Each story is like a separate car on a freight train. We may have gone one or two meters, or thousands, before realizing what was happening and where the mind has been.

- Come back to the breath and be aware of thoughts, as they arise and pass away.

- How freeing it is, when we are able to observe each thought (each box car) on a train of thought, and not be caught in everyone. We can watch the entire train come and go, whether it carries five or a hundred cars, without jumping on board.

- With each breath, let the body relax, and be at ease.

- Feel each breath, as it enters and leaves the body. Feel the stomach and chest rise, and fall, upon inhalation and exhalation.

- Slowly open the eyes and be aware of boxcars of thought. Beam Me Up Scotty

- Close the eyes, and let the body relax. Be comfortable.

- Imagine a beam that starts at the feet.

- As this beam covers the feet, let them relax.

- The beam can be like warm water, a ray of light, or the

beam in the transporter room of the Star Trek show, in which one part of the body after another slowly fades and evaporates into air.

- Now, feel the beam moving up the legs, pelvis and hips.

- Let the legs, pelvis and hips relax, melt away, and let go.

- Now, envision this beam as it moves along the front, side and back of the torso – the belly, chest, and back.

- Let the belly, chest and back slowly fade into a relaxed state.

- Now, imagine the beam as it moves up the hands, arms, and shoulders.

- Let the hands, arms and shoulders be at ease, let them float, or disappear.

- Now, envision this beam as it moves up the neck, the face, sides and top of the head.

- Let the neck, face, and sides of the head relax. Let them merge with the surrounding air.

- Scan the entire body, from the feet to the top of the head. If there are any areas that are tense, rigid, or tight, let them melt away in the beam.

- Come back to the breath. Feel the air surrounding the body.

- Slowly, begin to feel the top of the head, the face and neck.

- Notice the shoulders, arms, and hands.

- Bring awareness to the back, sides, chest and belly.

- Feel the hips, pelvis, legs and feet.

- Envision the beam (of water, or light), as the body evaporates, melts, or vanishes.

- Now, feel the air, as it enters and leaves the body.

- Put the hands on the belly, and feel it expand and contract with each breath.

- Notice the point of contact where the surrounding air is touching the skin.

- Slowly open the eyes and return to planet earth.

S.E.E.D.I.T.

(S = Senses, E = Emotions, E = Emptiness,
D = Desire, I = Intentions, T = Thoughts)

- Gently close the eyes, and relax the rest of the body.

- Feel the air surrounding the body, and the points at which it is contacting the skin.

- Become aware of breathing in and out, as the air enters and leaves the body. Let the body breathe naturally: no need to speed up or slow down.

- There is nowhere else to be and nothing to do. Be right here, right now.

- Every moment we are alive, we can utilize S.E.E.D.I.T.

- The shortcut of S.E.E.D.I.T. encompasses most anything we can experience.

- Keep following the breath and become aware of the senses, the S. in S.E.E.D.I.T. Notice sensations in the body, sounds, taste, and sight (when the eyes are open). Keep awareness on the senses, as they come and go.

- If sidetracked on another experience, return to the breath and the senses, or any one of the senses.

- Be aware of breathing in and breathing out.

- Now, include any emotions that come to attention. Be aware of the senses, and the E. in S.E.E.D.I.T. – emotions.

These may include sadness, joy, anger, fear, love, guilt, or anxiety.

- Like senses, there is no need to get rid of, or hold on to, any emotion. Be aware of what is there, and acknowledge it, as it arises and passes away.

- Breathe in and breathe out.

- If in a void, or a sense of emptiness is present, then identify it as such. The second E. in S.E.E.D.I.T. With emptiness, awareness of any specific emotion, sensation, thought or intention, is absent.

- Be aware of the breath, as it enters and leaves the body.

- Now, include any desires that come to attention - the D. in S.E.E.D.I.T. Wanting something, or someone, is desire. Having an urge for an object, or person, is desire. Wanting this moment to be different than it is everyone desire.

- Come back to the breath.

- Bring attention to the present experience and include any intentions that come into awareness. The I. in S.E.E.D.I.T. Intentions are similar to desires. An intention is something one wants, hopes for, or wishes to have happen. It is also a thought.

- Breathing in and breathing out, give full attention to the senses, emotions, emptiness, desires, and intentions - note which you are aware of at this moment. Watch them come and go.

- Now, include thinking, or thoughts. The T. in S.E.E.D.I.T. Was that a thought, or an emotion? What was I just

182

thinking? What sensation am I aware of? Was that another thought? Is that a desire? That's an interesting thought.

- Use S.E.E.D.I.T. to clarify and differentiate, what is coming into awareness, and what is happening, in the moment.

- If everything feels intense, or overwhelming, break it down with S.E.E.D.I.T. Is this a sense, an emotion, a feeling of emptiness, a desire, an intention, or a thought?

- Come back to the breath. Breathe in and breathe out.

- Be aware of the air around the body, and the points where it is felt.

- Slowly open the eyes and make it your intention to utilize S.E.E.D.I.T.

Space - The Final Frontier

- Look around the area in which you are sitting. There are things and people.

- Everything you see is a small fraction of the space surrounding them.

- The room we are in is contained within a larger space – a home, or building.

- The area outside the room is part of the atmosphere, which is a miniscule part of the space that surrounds earth.

- The space within which earth orbits is a tiny space, in a tiny galaxy that is surrounded by infinite space.

- Space within space within space.

- Now, close the eyes.

- Notice the air surrounding and touching the body.

- Feel the air as it enters and leaves the body with each breath.

- Notice the space between each breath, at the end of exhaling, and right before inhaling.

- Each breath brings us back to the space within.

- Like stars in space, and all the matter spinning, and moving through it, our sensations, emotions and thoughts arise and pass away within our awareness.

- When observed closely, with an open spacious mind, strong sensations, emotions, or thoughts, are not as big, or as important, as they may first appear to be.

- Let whatever is being experienced inside your inner solar system be as it is.

- You are not the objects that you are witnessing.

- Come back to the breath.

- Notice the space between each breath.

- Feel the air as it enters and leaves the body with each breath.

- Feel the air surrounding and touching the body.

- Slowly open the eyes and recognize the space in which we sit.

The Urge

- Gently close the eyes and let the hands and legs relax.

- Bring attention to the breath, as it fills the lungs, and then leaves the body.

- Scan the body, from head to toe, with awareness.

- Anywhere there is tension, tightness, or agitation, let it be and relax.

- Breathe in. Breathe out.

- Now, think of something you desire – food, freedom, sex, alcohol, drugs, peace, a job, a home, another place, or time.

- Notice how the object of your desire affects the body, and where it is most notable.

- Notice how the sensation of desire, affects emotions.

- What are the sensations and emotions, surrounding a specific urge, making you think about?

- What are you telling yourself about these urges and cravings? Recognize the moment, or point at which you first said, "I've got to have that."

- Urges come in waves. They can be strong, or just tickling your fancy.

- Desires, urges, or cravings, are all conditioned. They are based on past experiences, or in what we believe will provide momentary pleasure, contentment, or freedom from physical, emotional, and/or mental pain.

- Desire is not good or bad, but the time, attention, and focus we give to fulfill a specific desire, or urge, can control our life, and blind us to living in the present.

- By observing, and being aware of our urges, we then have greater choice in how, or if, we wish to pursue or respond to them.

- Being honest with ourselves about what we want, and why we want it, opens the door to more compassion for others – making sure we do not cause suffering or pain for others in order to fulfill our craving or desires.

- Return to the breath. Notice the air as it enters and leaves the lungs.

- Feel the air surrounding and embracing the body and slowly open the eyes.

Good Grief

- Gently close the eyes, settle in, and let the body relax.

- Be aware of the life-giving breath that enters and leaves the body.

- We take breathing for granted, unless we are having difficulty breathing.

- We take life for granted, unless we are having difficulty living.

- Return to the breath, as it enters and leaves the body.

- If any areas of tension, or discomfort, in the body come to attention, let it be.

- Pain, suffering and loss are part of being alive. This pain, and these losses, can be physical, emotional, and/or mental.

- Everything, and everyone, we care about, or are connected to, will someday leave, either by death, distance, or choice. It is impossible to permanently hold onto anyone, or anything.

- When loss occurs, it is painful. Grief is a natural response to loss. It hurts. Trying to avoid grief (like other emotions and thoughts) by pushing it away, keeping busy, or numbing out, doesn't work.

- Return to the breath, as it enters and leaves the body.

- Recall a time when you lost someone, or something, that was dear to you.

- Notice the feelings, sensations, and thoughts that arise when you remember that loss.

- Instead of avoiding them, or pushing them away, let yourself be with them in whatever manner they manifest themselves. Acknowledge what you are experiencing, and investigate it. Notice if there is shortness of breath in the chest, tightness in the throat or stomach. Notice if there is sadness, anger, guilt, love, or feelings of helplessness. Notice if there are thoughts trying to make sense of it, or figure it out.

- Give yourself permission to be with the pain of grief.

- Return to the breath, as it enters and leaves the body.

- Time doesn't heal all wounds, but time and attention eases the intensity and frequency of grief's impact.

- Ignoring loss and grief, is a sure way to inflict unconscious pain on the self and others.

- There is no need to immerse oneself in grief twenty four seven, but it can be beneficial to take a little time each day to acknowledge what has been lost; the reactions to that loss; and how one chooses to stay connected to, or understand, the person, or thing, that is lost.

- Return to the breath, as it enters and leaves the body. Slowly open the eyes. You are alive.

The Old One Two

- Gently close the eyes, and let the hands relax.

- Notice the air surrounding the body, and the areas on the skin where it is being touched by the air.

- Follow the air, as it makes its way into and out of the body, one breath at a time.

- Now, begin counting the breath, "one" when inhaling, and "two" upon exhale.

- At the beginning of the next in-breath, repeat "one", and while exhaling, repeat "two".

- Every time that you become aware of having lost count, or being caught in thought, start again with "one".

- It doesn't matter how many times you start over, or whether you make it through a complete in breath and out breath without the mind wandering.

- The very act of giving attention to the breath, moment to moment, helps develop concentration, which goes hand in hand with awareness.

- Breathe in. One. Breathe out. Two. Breathe in. One. Breathe out. Two.

- Keep coming back to the breath, as it enters and leaves.

- At the very instant you notice having been lost in thought, or forgetting whether you are breathing in or out, you have returned to awareness.

- Follow the air, as it makes its way into and out of the body, one breath at a time.

- Notice the air surrounding the body, and the areas on the skin where it is being touched by the air.

- Slowly open the eyes. Come back to the breath, and the old one two.

I Don't Like That

- Sit comfortably, let the hands relax, and gently close the eyes.

- Be aware of breathing.

- Notice anywhere in the body that is tight, tense, or uncomfortable.

- If you notice an area that doesn't feel good, don't try to get rid of the feeling, or sensation, just be aware of it and let it be.

- As we sit, notice any emotions, or thoughts, which are unpleasant – ones you want to get rid of, push away, or not acknowledge.

- Be aware of breathing.

- How many times a day do we say, "I don't like that"? What we don't like can be a sensation, an emotion, a thought, a person, or a situation.

- Telling ourselves we don't like something doesn't change the characteristics, or experience, of what it is we dislike.

- Instead of judging, or mentally pushing something in our awareness away, look at it closely and accept it for what it is.

- Be aware of breathing.

- By shining the light of awareness, and acceptance, on any emotion, sensation, or thought, it becomes apparent that what it is we don't like, is usually based on conditioning, and that it changes, shifts and fades away, when it's had some attention.

- Notice anywhere in the body that is tight, tense, or uncomfortable.

- If you notice an area that doesn't feel good, don't try to get rid of it, just be aware of it and let it be.

- Be aware of breathing.

- Slowly open the eyes, and continue learning how to accept what is, as opposed to how we want it to be.

Enough Already

- Close the eyes and breathe in the live-giving air that is always available.

- Each need for breath is fulfilled. Every breath is the right amount. There is enough air to go around.

- Breathe in and breathe out. Feel the air bringing everything you need, right now.

- Who we are, right now, is enough – nothing is lacking or missing.

- No matter what you've been told by others (family, friends, teachers, courts, relatives, or communities), you are enough. You are complete and whole.

- Breathe in and breathe out. Feel the air bringing everything you need, right now.

- Regardless of what you've told yourself, and made yourself believe, you are enough already.

- Being aware of the breath, and then sensations, emotions, and thoughts, can be the catalyst to understanding and accepting the self, as you are.

- Breathe in and breathe out. Feel the air bringing everything you need, right now.

- Acceptance, or being enough, doesn't mean we like everything we see, but we have all the necessary qualities needed to look at ourselves and choose to change or not.

- Without awareness, we continue striving to reach some goal, in order to be enough, and/or impress others that we are enough.

- Breathe in and breathe out. Feel the air bringing everything you need, right now.

- With awareness and insight into who we are, we develop insight and compassion for the conditioning we, and others, have perpetuated – that we are not enough.

- Each need for breath is fulfilled. Every breath is the right amount. There is enough air to go around.

- Open the eyes and breathe in the life-giving air that is always available.

Your Heart's Desire

- Gently close the eyes; let the hands, and legs relax, and feel the air surrounding the body, as it wraps you in its embrace.

- Notice the points where air is touching the skin – the hands, arms, face, and neck.

- Feel the air as it enters the body, one breath at a time – life-giving air.

- Settle in to the body, and notice any sensations, emotions, or thoughts that are present.

- Whatever is there is there. There's no need to push it away or try to hold on.

- Feel the air enter and leave the body.

- Now, ask yourself, "What do I want?" "What is my heart's deepest desire?"

- Notice whatever comes up – "I want to eat something." "I want this time to be over." "I want to stop drinking."

- Keep asking the question, what do you want beyond a temporary desire or moment? What do you want out of life?

- What is your intention? What do you want to see happen

most, right now, and in the future?

- What is your desire for others? What do you want most for family, friends, and lovers?

- Acknowledge whatever is your heart's desire – your deepest desire for this life.

- Come back to the breath, as you breathe in and breathe out.

- Notice the points where air is touching the skin – the hands, arms, face, and neck.

- Feel the air surrounding the body, as it wraps you in its embrace.

- Slowly open the eyes, and remind yourself of your heart's desire every day.

B.R.A.V.E.

(B = Before, R = Reacting, A = Access, V = Validate, E = Explore)

- Settle into the body, gently close the eyes, and let the hands and legs be at ease.

- Before reacting to any sensation, emotion or thought that arises, notice the breath with each inhale and exhale.

- Follow three breaths, one at a time, as they enter and leave the body.

- Now that you have access to the inner workings of the body and mind, see what happens.

- Acknowledge whatever sensation, or sense you are aware of.

- Recognize any emotions that make themselves known.

- Validate every thought that comes into consciousness.

- Look closely at any senses, sensations, emotions, or thoughts that arise, and explore each one. Use the light of awareness like a microscope.

- See if there are any connections between one sensation and another; between an emotion and another; between one thought and another that preceded it.

- Observe any correlations between the senses, emotions and thoughts. Does one affect another?

- Be brave. Don't shy away from anything. Look at everything.

- Now, follow three breaths in a row, as they enter and leave the body.

- Slowly open the eyes. Don't stop being B.R.A.V.E.

Body Anchor

- Close the eyes, place the feet on the floor, and let the hands relax.

- Let the body set anchor, right where it is, right now.

- With each breath, let gravity pull the feet, ankles, legs and hips towards the earth.

- With each breath, allow the hands, wrists, arms, and shoulders to relax, and let go.

- With each breath, the back, pelvis, belly, and chest are released.

- With each breath, the neck, face and head are at ease.

- The entire body is upright, but grounded through the feet.

- If there is tension, tightness, or discomfort anywhere in the body, let it be.

- Like a ship in a stormy sea, let the body drop anchor.

- There is nowhere to go, nothing to do, and nothing to prove.

- Breathe in. Breathe out. Breathe in. Breathe out.

- Observe any of the senses, sensations, emotions, or

thoughts, as they appear and float away.

- Sink into the body. It is your home. Wherever you are, there it is.

- Feel the air, as it enters and leaves the body.

- Feel the feet on solid ground.

- Feel the air that surrounds and feeds the body.

- Slowly, open the eyes and set anchor whenever needed.

The Casket

- Close the eyes, settle the body, and feel the air, as it enters and leaves the body.

- Scan the body, from head to toe, and anywhere there is tension, or tightness, let it be and relax.

- Feel the breath, as it enters and leaves the body.

- Imagine, if you had recently stopped breathing and died, and you are at your own funeral.

- Your body is lying in the casket. What do you see? Who is there?

- What was, or is, your life about?

- If there is anything you could have, or can, change, what would it be?

- What would you say about yourself?

- Now, leave the casket, and the room, and come back to the breath.

- Feel yourself breathing in and out.

- Today, or tomorrow, or decades from now, this life will end.

- What matters most? What are your deepest intentions?

- Every life matters, including yours.

- Scan the body, from head to toe, and anywhere there is tension, or tightness, let it be and relax.

- Slowly open the eyes, and feel the air as it enters and leaves the body.

- You are alive at this moment. The time to start living, with awareness, is now.

Birds of a Feather

- Let the body relax and the eyes close.

- Sit comfortably.

- Feel the touch of the air surrounding the body on the skin.

- Be aware of the air, as it enters the body.

- The air we breathe is the same air that makes up the sky.

- The air we breathe is the same air that is blown, like clouds, by the wind.

- The air we breathe is the same air in which birds fly.

- Sensations, emotions and thoughts are similar to birds in the sky. They come in a variety of shapes, and sizes. Some stay in one place and move slowly, while others race through space, from one point to another.

- Let the mind be an open sky and thoughts be like birds as they come and go.

- When a thought enters awareness, notice when it is there, what shape it takes, and where it goes.

- It is impossible to change the kind of bird, or thought, that becomes conscious, or make it fly, or move at a different speed. It comes and goes at its own pace.

- If you find you have been drifting with a thought, like a feathered friend riding the wind, than the moment you realize it, you are once again the sky of awareness.

- There is no other place to be. There is nothing else to do. Just sit and watch the thoughts come and go.

- Slowly, bring attention back to the breath - the same air that is in the sky. The same air in which the birds fly.

- Be aware of the air, as it enters the body.

- Feel the touch of the air surrounding the body on the skin.

- Open the eyes slowly. Whenever life feels confined, or closed in, remember the sky, the consciousness within which different birds of thought come and go.

Belly Jelly

- Let the body relax and the eyes close.

- Sit comfortably.

- Be aware of the air, as it enters the body.

- Follow a breath as it enters the nose, goes down the throat and into the lungs. Notice the belly rise and fall with each breath.

- Breathe naturally, as the breath comes and goes. Let the body relax; completely relax.

- Gently put one or both hands on the belly, and be aware of them rising and falling with each breath.

- Allow the hands to completely relax and notice the point where they contact the belly.

- Let the belly soften, and be at ease. Like a bowl of soft giggly jelly.

- Bring attention back to the breath, as the belly rises and falls.

- Follow the breath as it enters the nose, goes down the throat and into the lungs and then returns from the lungs, through the throat and out the nose or mouth.

💭   Feel the touch of the air surrounding the body on the skin.

💭   Open the eyes slowly. Whenever feeling tense, or uneasy, bring awareness to the belly and let it relax and soften.